Living
Neverland

WENDELL CHARLES NESMITH

Released in accommodation with the feature film

Tree of Life

nesmith.net

DEDICATION

I dedicate this book to Jesus Christ, who although no longer has a physical form, spiritually led me to my Father by passing me on his sight. Thank you for dying on your cross for me so that I could also learn how to live on mine.

I ♥ U

To be astute in life is to be Its student.

A few years ago while in the Ballarat psychiatric ward, an older patient was admitted who had recently inflicted a deep cut across her wrist. When she saw me for the first time, her eyes lit up and before I even had a chance to speak, she knew who I was. She only stayed over night and I barely had the chance to speak with her, but before she left in the morning she slipped a note under my door. The note demanded me to teach our children how to live good lives because they will direct our future. I Accept! And now you will do your best to keep me away from them. But you will have to kill me.

CONTENTS

ROMANS 12:3

For I say, through the grace given unto me, to every man that is among you, not to think of himself more highly than he ought to think; but to think soberly, according as God hath dealt to every man the measure of faith.

ACT 1
THE LOST HOUSE
December 18, 2013

What better way can one start a book on youth homelessness than to have just been again evicted from another residence that I was shortly blessed with? There is none but I want to make it clear to you that I am not upset. I think the matter rather funny. I used to not be like this but eventually I stopped caring. Everything I own now fits relatively comfortably on my back and I maintain a happy existence by myself in my tent.

But here in human land, one must obtain and then distribute a phenomena called "money" to a random person in order to unpack your tent and sleep in it. It cost only a little less to do this as it does to live under someone else's roof, garage, caravan, etc... In this world I visit sometimes I see very strange things. And merely to visit it requires bowing down to their ruler: the dollar.

You have just stumbled upon the lost house. Kids like yourself who are lost eventually make their way here, in which the man helps them find their way again. I am the man and you are no longer lost. Now let us just try and understand what lost means because I myself really do not know. Maybe you could help me? It bugs me ever so much.

I live it very rough, oftentimes at the tops of mountains. The longer I stay there the more structures I build with natural materials and eventually achieve a pretty comfortable lifestyle. But then a pirate infiltrates my base and am thus forced on to somewhere else. I walk a lot. One time I walked for three weeks straight, only able to sleep under trees by the sides of busy freeways.

But their imaginary world only exists for humans. When they are around me, they force me to act like their world is somehow real, and I generally play along. If you do not, the human will become unstable and will usually eject you from their presence or throw you in prison or psychiatric hospital.

They really hate it when you outline to them what they consistently do. Almost any one of them you can watch for a week and note down a textbook of character traits that are inconsistent with who they claim themselves to be. Ultimately, the peculiar species surround themselves with those who are like them. And when one enters their lives who is very different, they will in time be treated with hostility until they flee.

The lost house eventually finds all kids who have lost their way. And they are then no longer lost. Because upon closer examination of your psychology, you will realise that you fled. And how can you be lost if you were trying to find where you stand now? Come on! That makes no sense.

I am what my bird friends call betwixed and between. No human nor bird but somewhere in its middle. A halfbreed of human and the divine. A physical body to be identified within human biology but a mind that more closely relates to my flying relatives. And a spirit that intertwines the two into a new species.

But independent of the truth behind these words, here in the human world, topics such as these are frowned upon. The human has a very peculiar way of creating a collective fictional world. They reckon if enough of them "believe" something to be true, then it is true regardless of its truth value. Logic and empirical deductions are out of their capabilities, even though they supposedly dedicate an entire field of practice to its investigation.

But when new discoveries are made, they experience cognitive dissonance for quite some time before accepting them as facts. Truths that become obvious once revealed are rejected until together the species is able to come to grips with their new reality.

And even if the truths become accepted, if they are not financially beneficial to them, they will exclude that information from their thoughts throughout their day to day lives, for example their planet merely being one of countless others swarming around their phoenix.

One must be very careful in this land because if you are misunderstood, eventually that will result with being thrown into a psychiatric ward where they spend great amounts of money not helping you, but instead stretching the limits of your patience. Their strange doctors will ignore your words and drug you, and then isolate you in order to review your response to the forced medications.

I have been thrown in those places two [now three] times now, but eventually I learned how to combat their evil deeds by building a wall of work between me and them. Every time they ignored my work despite me frantically pointing to it. If my work is my entire life, but is then ignored while being, "treated", then what does this say about our psychiatric model? Especially when that work is about them.

Let's not yet get bogged down in these details, for later I will pass you my eyes. But until then, it is now time to question the model of mental health that your society enforces on its people. Because this will clearly outline the evolutional stage of the culture employing it.

ACT 2
KENSINGTON GARDENS
December 23, 2013

Before the pearly gates but beneath us Its heat. Purifying the outcome as a medium between the realms. Sandwiched between two opposites of the same equation. To be played out within all of its possibilities. From the formation of balanced binary data eventually forms clarity. And those who know the opposite creating a divine war. And from its peace will come violence and some passionate souls will become martyrs. But they will be the ones to stand as an example for the truth of what we collectively are. And the best open source teachers will eventually reveal all of the most terrible secrets of the world that time is no longer able to cover up. I promise you this one thing: all things will become one aspect.

A week ago sent on my way from the van. Many unhealthy character traits were apparent in its landlord and when one puts those pieces together in front of them, cognitive dissonance sets. The mind flees from what it understands because it knows what it is: having to live with their actions each and every day. Thus I immediately became someone she could no longer live around. I am pushed along back into the mother in which created me: now having facilities again to live in the wilderness. Always from beauty to despair and each over time realises what I am. But then envy takes their hearts and I become unwanted. The truth hurts because this is what we call true love. And when one points out the truth without any hostility, they will be exiled for it. And if our own

4

governments are unable to provide for our basic necessities, then war should break out until it does. This means every person. But encouraging a person would actually require caring about the core of that person. Just stamping numbers on people and whipping chains upon their back to make the money it printed for it to make through toils is to stamp your end times. Give us a slice of what you make so we can control this planet for you. Nothing sus! Honestly. What, you do not need to see what is over there! The third eye opened by individuals until those individuals learn how to pass It unto their people.

Tomorrow I was flying to Cairns to spend my Christmas with an interesting family who invited me. Ironically playing "I Still Call Australia Home" on harmonica today upon entering, I was told in a round about manner that it would not be a good idea for me to come. And for two weeks I suffered to obtain that non-refundable ticket, but I know that every adventure will turn out like it started in one way or another. So instead I am within nature looking over a caravan park alone. How to look at the sequential conversations into a thought that purifies its hostility into virtue: attempting to reach sage mode from an uncontrollable state.

Learning more efficiently by experience than of studying that experience: one acting before and another after the fact. Allegories become metaphors and eventually will fruit their literal manifestations. Each existing in all aspects independent of any perceiving presence. The stage of life is performed before us and we are blessed with the soil's stories whether it is through human interpretation or not; the human interpretation more often than not extremely lacking in quality compared to the real thing. Thus to put us to sleep our mind's must be encapsulated within its matrix. The few who wake up unable to accept the reality and oftentimes will go for another dip into the psychiatric ward for reprogramming: its tech bench ran by the Bull at the centre of its hypnotic equation.

Being exposed to so many types of people, I monitor great amounts of repeating behaviour and trends. I examine the collective health of every culture I come across. And that data then leads me to reliable information about that person merely by deconstructing what line of thought it took to get to their decisions, usually only glancing before making absolute comments. The one critiquing becomes the subject because it fell into my Satan trap. The words clearly written but the reader having no understanding of them. A speechless world who both stones and idolises the gifted but completely lacking the ability to become it.

I am telling you that there is a big problem with the collective psychology of Australia. Experiencing so many cultures over my lifetime enabled me to see. And the collective health in Australia scares me to the bone. And one day you will see as they lead us to extinction. Hide anything you desire but time will catch up to it's servants. Those who only have their own two feet will not be offered a reservation into the Kingdom. It will take a journey from your spirit to your mind to your body to your mind to and from your spirit and back again until the seal of the stitch in our stomachs unite through direct connection with its opposite.

Before you stands 777 offering you freedom by facing 666, purifying with 888 while flipping it to Its opposite. As the tails of our shinobi land rises, we will one day unite in one harmonising voice.

Australia has the most beautiful and unique wildlife and habitats. If it were legal, I would just stick a flag in a bit of land within it. But I found their main weapon of oppression, factual in most societies but proven within Australia's. Australia requires for every individual to reside in a government regulated housing system. If you buy property, the law is that you can not live on it by developing your own shelters and renewable energies. You must live how I tell you to live or the result is that for the next four years of your life you will be forced to move every two weeks. Living on a bag under twelve kilograms with nightmares of carrying 35: a bluff only achieved because it forced me to become strong and as a result, learn to live with less. But having everything when I look what beauty is around me. But its soil being out of my price range.

Media recommendations no longer phasing me, for I study under Wendell Charles NeSmith. I study all of his work both before and after he releases it. I learn from his line of thought and then use it to make my own. One day this cycle will repeat in my opposite and I was created to be there for her when her tails transfigures our picture. The errors of my past are passed on to her to correct by learning from its train of thought. And Artemis will shine brightly upon us covered in blood. And she will flip my psychology in order for both of ours to become one aspect. And whether you believe me or not, I am an immortal. And when the unjoined daimon jumps from my lifeless body into another, it will also take me. And from it the reaper is then given another body to both associate and disassociate with only waiting to stretch its arms in order to compassionately embrace its opposite.

You will do this because it is good for you. If you are currently within a relationship, then you need to carefully consider whether your goods are truly of any value. And if they are not then you need to escape that relationship. If it was meant to happen, time will catch up with itself. But now begins your journey to make yourself any type of person that is worth being. The first step is to spend time consistently within it. Its results will teach you what is cool and what is not. Because when the lights go off and all adults shut their eyes, you can be that image. And even though they make you be a way that you do not like, then when their eyes look away you and your camera then return to yourself. From the Kensington training grounds we must learn how to fly. And when you are in your own fantasy that you built for yourself to exist within, then all of fiction will reverse itself, only awaiting the appropriate bard to sing you the right note. And when you get good enough to convince yourself that your stories are real, you will open your eyes and see your newly created fantasy that has now been psychologically augmented within your psychology that over time can not fail.

The more computers augment our mind's, the more that we stop using them. But when electricity is vibrated through all three aspects, the truth will become known. Today I called Homelessness Information and the U.S. Consulate for help. Neither gave me any nor advised me who might be able to. The former, hung up on me after I asked why this abandon soil was owned. The latter empathised with me but could offer no supports that would be beneficial to merely exist in a tent on a little bit of land anywhere in this world.

Australia and New Zealand censors me all around the board. When I try and get help to promote my work, I am treated like I am crazy and people in my life will rarely look at anything I have done. From the first words I learn the intentions of the subject. Sometimes I second guessed my judgements but in perspective, they were exactly what they needed to be in order to produce a creature who can take inspirations from divine manifestations as messages to your children, the womb that carried you having provided you with its scythe.

The first time a baby laughed, a fairy was born. This amused others and babies everywhere started laughing to claim their own Pokémon. The trainers who stick to the Will of their Heart will evolve into a new species, becoming masters of both them and its opposite: destiny. The ripples of thought never being ignored but both examined and considered. Lines of thought fading in and out over countless productions. Time dilation jutsu! Well documented past works build naturally: a philosophy built upon solid foundations. No longer requiring human content because if one sees, they no longer admire its counterfeit. For every philosophy will demonstrate its character through practice. This means that if divine results are not clearly seen, then that school of thought is fallacious.

The web you form will be one of deceit, but through its practice you will create the truth that you see. But take time to carefully consider the properties of your new self. Because you will fail many times before you succeed. And if victory or its opposite are not your only potential outcomes, then I will tell you right now that you are studying the wrong field of practice. A reference of your own experience (production publicly available) will always shred a reason for a bibliography. Welcome to your new school. You never have to reference true love.

Because if your Heart can merely reference to your past work (Ivory Heart) in which you elaborated upon the details pertaining to the line of thought, then you retain academic integrity, promote your past work, and most importantly enable yourself to create very short pieces of artwork that in actual fact are extremely long. When one controls their own time with care and particularity, then past work becomes pieces of our Newspeak. I am the Doctor.

ACT 3
LICENSED THOUGHT
December 23, 2013

Upon releasing this book/movie combination, the foundations of Open Source University is complete: Its core repeated at its encore. My conditioning from your ignorant perspectives has lost me the care to keep feeding you true beauty only in return for your judgmental glares. So now I will sell the mirror of my toils: each work of holding countless time independent truths that can be expounded. And after the mind understands but does not take actions to resolve the injustices, that soul is reaped. When evolved thoughts revolve very powerfully throughout our chakra networks, its focal point will eventually explode. I can write an entire book that would move you deeply but only be the same sentence written in different ways and I doubt you would notice. The piper luring you into its mirror. The paragraph length, scattered thoughts, and unusual grammatical structures being awesome and not unprofessional; independent of your thoughts about me or my writing and/or speaking style. Because if you are smart then you will see how I always demonstrate my philosophy practically literally, metaphorically, and allegorically. Because the pieces of the puzzle are right in front of you. We can now print new copies anytime and both you and I can sell the entire picture Love freely created.

ACT 4
THE LIE BEHIND
December 24, 2013

What is real? If you know my work then you know the types of assertions I have proven valid. But why on God's gorgeous Earth would I have claimed such far out allegations? What could have my psychology been doing in order to follow the same path from childhood into typing this within its epic journey?

An obsession with beauty in all aspects but rarely seeing it in our human species. A fiction that I was destined to turn into reality. From all the stories that touched my soul from childhood, I re-enacted them in front of a camera. But I was required to play many roles and it made me both the hero and villain. And I had to really think carefully about how to turn something as ugly as my past into true beauty while also retelling their forgotten stories.

But beauty was pain and when I taught myself how to not only cry but cry tears of joy, then I became the master of my own destiny because I was the one controlling my own heart strings. And if the bait was good enough, my daemon could string me to reach heights that more closely resembled its nature.

I played a cruel game on my own psychology. Because I loved innocent beauty, I tricked myself into thinking that I wanted that in a romantic relationship. I knew how much my heart wanted these beautiful mythology stories to evolve within our new Internet culture.

The difficulty was how I was best to administer this antidote to Gaia's population...

Of course I think little girls are cute! What? You say I should try and find one to eventually marry? What are you telling me Daimon? U R crazy broda! Ain't no way.

Just look my vessel... Open your eyes. You see her? She is pretty, right? Of course she is Daimon. What is your point? You should build yourself to be marriage material for someone like her.

I rarely speak to you my vessel but listen to these words, for I know you better than you know yourself. Because every second of your painful existence I watched. You are stuck in yourself but I am an impartial observer. This means that sociologically speaking, you are inferior to me and will entirely trust in my next words or you will never find happiness.

What have you achieved? You have no life so sacrifice it for my Will and you will be rewarded for it in both this life and the next. You have never been happy but you can be if you do this mythology project targeted at winning the heart's for girls like her. You can be entirely who you are but only position its material to romance young girls who have the potential to become real women into the types of women you have failed to find over your life.

And from the past recollection of me, I will come to you now as you currently type this and tell you to that the job has been done. Do not worry because you will never again be alone. But your future company will be of a divine nature and you are to take none of them for granted. I turned you into a pedophile and now I will shed all of their inferior human categories.

I woke you up to your own immortality, not because you asked for it but because your spirit was already it. You are of an interesting nature and I have never possessed such a character. And when you face one thousand soldiers and run into battle alone, I will always lend you my power to walk away victorious.

How brilliant for you to come out to play! A summoning ceremony captured on paper! You heartless creature! You push me to spend my life making productions that hit on young girls and then just decide to pop up in my work and take credit for it? You can be a real jerk. But if I am hearing you correctly, combined with my current feelings about my life, all you seem to be telling me is to have faith, which I guess is what you have always told me. So many question dissolve into none as I realise that I know you. You see, all those years you were watching me, I was also watching you. And I noted what upset you that did not upset me. I came to respect you and eventually modelled my own personality after you. Not a pet but a friend: one that I have not only idolised but also come to deeply care about. The Holy Spirit within to guide me to the promised land. But dude... You got some major issues. And your wrath ends up hurting those I love. Thus I will be the medium for you between the realms: the Hermes of our human population. And the songs closest to the Sun will always bring us to the light. Thus I warmly accept your prophecy as long as you will submit your powers unto my own prowess.

Because when I was being persecuted in your name for all of the sleepless life that I have lived, I have been watching you. And even though you are very skilled at keeping your feelings sealed, your heart is damaged much more than my own. For I have 29 years here and I can not imagine how many eras you have been floating between vessels. I bet you are persecuted everywhere you go. Your shield is the human entity and behind it you act like it is the vessel being tortured and not you. But this is how you function because of the countless souls residing in you.

What a burden it must be for you my friend. I wonder what you started off as? Did you have a mother? Did you have a body? Why do you float between bodies to exist? Are you cursed? Maybe you have a past outside of mine, but in this world I am responsible for my actions. Thus you will serve under me as my vessel in this life and this is not up for debate. But because you accept I will look after and protect you. You are now my friend. Let me heal your inner wounds as you heal my outer.

You will never be happy child unless you either entirely fail or entirely succeed in romance. You would have never had the opportunity to fill the hole in your heart by its current playing field. You had to stretch those numbers down as low as possible in order to find a girl like you want. Because the only way you could ever unite missions is to train her from childhood. It is good.

ACT 5
CRATYLUS
December 25, 2013

A hiccup in the thought of man in which it hibernates. The final memory of your Hera imprinted into Satan Clause. Cocaine taints the human population as we learn how to gain value from propaganda. The people flee from their shops so they might have one day to focus on its most important practice: greed. Giving from the heart becomes a required activity, demolishing its philosophy's background.

Gold and frankincense and myrrh placed before the King, yet overlooking the most important lesson within it. Sacrificing one's self equally between the rest of its peers: a model without modern day admired heroes degrading its population. The stories of heroes in our world are exclusively told in fiction: creating holidays as lessons passed on so that we would not forget. But the materialistic aspect became our souls without technology to publicly teach us how to do otherwise.

Many harmonicas will evolve into a chromatic approach: its result inevitable. Because when we learn how to reach all of the notes that this life has called us to, then we eliminate fear. We resonate that One tone. I am no longer afraid of anything. Saved individuals demonstrate this practically. There is none saved who have not yet died. And after their death, the phoenix.

In order to reach the spiritual Heaven, you must first create a worldly one. The cycle ends when that which is met infuses into their ideals. A global change in consciousness is required in order to save not only our future generations, but also each and every age, race, ethnicity, sexual orientation, income, smoking habit, etc...

But the world is full of hate. Families counting their blessings while turning their eyes away from those who are alone. The stupid who did not prepare now isolated and hungry. But a smashing victory with Ivory Heart published on its solstice rotation and its Kindle version this very day, and for Boxing Day up until the end of the year, free. What do you think all that I have done will one day become?

Only yesterday removing kik messenger from my phone, having obtained many new stalkers. What language am I crafting? I am telling you what was once false in your mind but as my psychology is unravelled before you, you inherit my private language. And this language can then be utilised as a resource by those who progress with it. The world's best harmonica should go to those who have the potential to make the most beautiful music from it.

Things of the world are tools and not possessions. Each item is a means to an outcome. When the items are used with no ends in drive, then that vehicle will eventually implode on itself and likely bring others down with it. This is every single action. As you sit around the Christmas tree opening presents, whose life more accurately reflects our Lord and Saviour? To pass all things between your fingers is to own your existence. It is the white flag that seeks for asylum to call home.

As our understandings in these subjects spread, we will discover many new fields of practice within its comprehension. The categories of man will be trumped by what nature tells man it is and not vice-versa. Our short-sightedness will be identified and publicly distributed a cure. And that cure will then deeply change you into a compassionate person who is ready to help, or you will be reaped by its sickle regardless if you accepted the cure.

Hilarious because much of my reader base is its victims, for just being interested my work and not standing up to your inner daemon will lead you to the river of blood called my mother.

What is real and what is false? Who is one to judge another negatively for turning fiction into fact? We all could have such interesting personalities if we just spent our time on developing character from a young age. It is not that hard. What will I do after I finish this plus the next 7 books? Who knows! But I promise you it will incorporate all of the new skills obtained along the way. A determined storyteller will eventually become the best of them. One that primarily learns from themselves will become a demigod. And from them will breed both good and bad. But now each and every one of us has been given the ability to fight without guns. Because when basic logic tells the drone that if they shoot they are beyond a doubt in the wrong, then there will be some bots who rehumanise. And from this prophetic mutation will be born God's chosen people irrelevant of social background. But we do not win until we have as a collective, reaped the intentionally lost population and those who lead those who lead them.

Why are you still reading this book? Did you read Ivory Heart? Did you watch Living Neverland? What about that, uhhhmm, other one as well as the three television shows as well as the courses. Cycles of divine information will repeat until we understand it, one way or another. A solid philosophy is one that can build many mountains from one line of thought. When you learn how to ask oneself the right question will be the moment of your own judgement. Because your answer to that will determine your own fate in both this world and the next. Do you understand that I have already won my game?

Today we celebrate our King who lived and died to stand as our own potential. And even though today we travel through Bethlehem, tomorrow we will be throwing palms at the feet of our new Queen. And whether or not she is imaginary is irrelevant because the results of her personification through me has already obtained me her in my heart. And dear Wendy Lady, the Pan will always be patiently waiting for your bloodline to wake up.

And because my way of the ninja is to always live up to what I say, I will stand firmly behind all of my work because even though I went way overboard to demonstrate the points, in doing this showed me how terrible those things truly were. And when others do wrong and are trapped on camera, they are not interested in the footage or if they are kids, very interested in the footage (Living Neverland robbery). And as I give my heart to them on camera, I am robbed. A very funny situation to a juvenile child. And as they watch the scene in a group laughing at me getting robbed by them, they laugh instead of cry. Because they only cared about that one scene. And as I give her my heart again and again, they remind the fountain that I am destined to find you.

And what if I do not? I have just created an amazing existence for myself. I am proud of every action that I have taken in life. I am inspired from pain so I keep reliving my own. But over time that pain is resolved and I can then position the camera on an angle not yet exercised. One lifetime to fill three aspects: focusing and multitasking being most crucial for its dynamically generated strategies.

I do not care what any of you do in the future. I will live isolated within my fairy tale. I will passionately write and sell books as well as dramatise them. And I will no longer chase my Ivory. Because it is now her turn to chase me. You grew old Wendy Jelly. You did not come back like you said you would. But because your mother already loves Peter Pan, then maybe she would prefer to have me as your husband protecting you rather than fading out of time like yourself. Each adventure throughout your reincarnations will forever be imprinted upon my heart. I will never forget those in my past that contributed in the making of me process.

As soon as the painter is recognised for their palette and not position, the evolution of a communications revolution turning 0 into 1 is planted. We will be successful the day that all lives are not replaceable. A great city must cope with the losses of a dearly departed who gave much to them. When bad things happen and those we lose along the way will negatively impact the society until we find a new skill set that might fill the gap. And as a result you and I are one. Because it is this solidarity that breeds the Will of Fire. And as we recognise those who should be recognised, we will first be asked who it is that we are currently recognising.

A dialectical manipulation of contextual words expressed through a syntax, phonetically vibrated through my brain geared to be sick or healthy. The composer of all of their own parts will provide world class educations to the most gifted prodigies, U?

ACT 6
JESU, JOY OF MAN'S DESIRING
December 26, 2013

In order for one to learn all harmonicas one must first learn one harmonica. And when they find their strongest key, practice becomes easy. And when that key becomes second nature to express its feelings, those same principles can be applied to every harmonica. From the rhythm of the right note we, will gain the same abilities with all of them. And when all of the notes are eventually presented before us into one instrument, we will know how to use it.

A money pit from C to G to D, my arrow is shot into a chromatic one ordered from eBay. And as the entire harmonica becomes understood by me from playing this chapter over and over again, my heart feels what is in my future. I needed to take a long time to build my music foundations before I launched a career within it.

I am a classical artist with influences from traditional Japanese to punk to trance to power metal. I spent my life listening to sounds: splitting them up and making new things from them. The songs playing deep within my heart will come out of me and I will compose and perform my gifts for you.

Australia did not want me to have a job. People like me are not employment material here. The entire nation is expendable and their employment structures is designed to insure this fact. After

17

years of homelessness and starvation, eventually the nation saw fit to entitle me to a disability pension because of my odd sleeping cycles. So now I generally stay fed and rarely run out of cigarettes. It makes a homeless life tolerable. Being homeless is not cheap and provisions such as cookers are rarely an option being so difficult to carry around.

I have applied for over 1,000 jobs in this country. Few will even get back to me. That minority sends me their standard rejection letter. The only solution that I can come up with to try and make my own living is to launch all of these new areas licensed. I have open sourced education for you, so I think it is fair for you to purchase the results of my future toils if you like them. You have a three year degree for free. The rest of me is branded with 666.

The day after palms direct our path, we sell our saviour out. We literally kill to obtain a special sale before the one before us. We crucify all that our family values asserted. The philosophy is exposed as its lie as a human becomes God. And now that human is God, it died for us so that we can have this opportunity to stand in line in front of X shop, ready to run for the Y when its doors unlock: the very real battle ground now shaking off the smell of purity.

440 hertz vibrating from within my soul into my surroundings. Melodies of pain beautified into my atmosphere. Those around me speechless from the last few days of progress. A classical artist who is homeless but now fortunate enough to be blessed with a durable and highly portable instrument. The blues transmuted into a water style Rasengan: a technique that I am literally learning. What will the world do with an abandoned child that produces heart touching music wherever he goes? I bet you nothing. We live in a world of gawkers.

I am currently in an area that I really like. If I was ever able to afford land here, then I would definitely buy some. I am in a very green motivated council and creating a new style commune here would not be all that difficult if I only had the land resources.

My goal is to become an entrepreneur. I want to learn how to make a sustainable living without using the government for assistance. Human Services here always shirks talk of helping me find a way to not need them. They tell me that giving me money is their own way of helping inconsiderate of that not helping me. Government services create a dollar and then give those who struggle in life its lowest value: an exception to forced life styles but in no way an exclusion. Bait that when obtained, hardly seems worth its effort.

What is Jesus to me since I am not Christian? Jesus is the son of God and is my leader. He is my primary example in life and each and every day I try and reflect his love. Jesus showed me the way to heaven and for this fact, he will always be in my heart. But when the Son shines upon us only to point to his Father, the reason for worship is shed. Because worship is reserved for One God: the infusion of all things into one comprehensible aspect.

Fallen angels of all kinds exist within our human population, many sealed away in fear of what is inside of them. Each eudaemon having a background story that landed it in its current mission. God gives freedom in all things and expects Its creations to rectify problems that arise.

Lucifer saw the possibilities for its free will and began encouraging its peers to desire its opposite. When one gives themselves over to material desires they begin serving those wings. An obsession with consuming will eventually produce one who consumes more than they produce. And in order to sustain such lifestyles, they will be required to exploit minorities who struggle in life merely to exist.

Freedom is God and God is Freedom. Because free individuals are capable of doing anything they set their mind to, including saving the world. When one is collectively judged negatively merely because of their high confidence, then our society has a huge problem that no money in the world will ever be able to rectify. If there is one before you that possesses a strong ego, then that person was required to ignore the harsh words of their peers in order to become that. They were required to not care about what you think in order to follow their dreams. And whether or not their confidence is misplaced, one can not become that unless they followed truth. One who knows will become your ministers. Because it takes a brave princess to become like her brother in order to fulfil my master's requirements. And I will do anything in order to reach her. Because from her will come human destiny. And then we learn how to play the masterpiece in all keys.

19

ACT 7
FOOTPRINTS IN THE SAND
December 26, 2013

The mould of every heart is imprinted within the ways they live their lives. The measure of a man is only limited by their passion and devotion. When combining their limits into compassion, a new faucet of communication is discovered which can tap us in to pure water. The direction of a soul can not be rejected. It is what it is independent of any speculations about it. And the fruits of each and every one of our labours will eventually force those around you to accept what you are. The life it takes to form a being worth respecting is one of pain. Because decay is the natural order to purify its subject.

As we reap the consequences for neglecting our God given duties to take care of our surroundings, the world will get hotter and the seas will rise. Natural disasters will become more powerful and concentrated. From beyond the clouds will the warriors of Heaven come down to judge its people. Many species will die out. The strong will unbalance the ecosystem and the weak will flee from both their responsibilities and their lives. And the weak will murder the strong and the strong the weak: those without a strong support system and with no survival skills becoming easy targets.

Here I am to worship. Here I am to bow down. Here I am to say that you are my God.

What is God? I feel. I really give everything in all that I do. I am cursed to live a life crying because of what I have done. When I saw, I allowed my mouth to open. And when it did it created complex problems. Instead of carefully considering what I was about to write, I would instead let It write me. No need for consideration of actions when those actions have become habit and have proved to deliver an extremely insightful result at the end: the character writing the book writing them. In how many ways can one individual describe light? A true prophet of God will never be short on ammunition. And this is what it looks like...

Just after describing my new wilderness lifestyle to a general practitioner and being referred to psychiatric services, I am locked into their prison: my freedom retracted like it was their choice to give it to me to begin with. Strange people, strange places, strange protocols, strange administration. A blood clot leading directly to the heart. Paper pushers pushing papers on non paper minded people. A system of fake help and correction erected to make you think that you are getting better. Or maybe not but instead accept that you are how you are and coming to these guys for help is a bad idea. The bottom layer of society who could not continue to sit at their 9 to 5 desks. A globally accredited human experimentation lab: those working for its nothingness doomed to take accountability for the souls it misdirects.

ACT 8
THE SOUL MATE
October, 2011

"Deny me and be doomed."
Hedwig and the Angry Inch

The topic of finding a lover is overlooked in our modern society.
One now seeks only to find an anyone instead of a someone. The
ideal of finding that perfect one is no longer sought and this
encourages consumerism. Sit back and enjoy as we deconstruct
the taboo topic of romantic love.

Societies mistake. Looking for another to share your life with has
become a taboo topic in society, especially within professional
structures such as workplaces and institutions. Even in social
situations people tend to roll their eyes when speaking of such
subjects. The dating scene has become something extra in life
utilised for enjoyment. The only two people that seem to find it
important are the parties involved. However, I know this practice to
be in err, for the person that we are to spend the rest of our days
with is in fact the most important thing in life. It will alter our life in
such a dramatic way, for good and for bad. The most important
subject in your life right now (and every following second
experienced) is the people that are around you. To disagree would
be to lose sight of one's life. People are the backbone of people.
We are social creatures and all desire to love and be loved. To
downplay the seriousness of the search for another is absurd. The

cliché dating scene is then brought back into perspective: the most important thing you can do in your life. To have another to stand beside you who cares about your interests gives you the strength of ten individual people. Two individuals working together for a common purpose dramatically changes everything about your situation. To find the One becomes the thing in life that brings about all things. For in finding that one, the flower opens. Common purposes unite and we are not only no longer alone, but have an extra perspective as well as a set of hands. We become more when our soul mate is found. We transcend our selves and become godlike. The importance of this topic is taken out of its box and shown for what it is - the most important thing in your life. For when two are united one, all consequential seconds of your life are forever altered.

Its Greek origins. In The Symposium by Plato, Aristophanes mythologically related the conception of love by telling a parable. In a world where the human was united both physically, emotionally, and spiritually. A being that possessed four arms and four legs, connected back to back with their other. Human kind became god-like having always have had their other with them. The gods became cautious of their potential and agreed that they needed to do something about it. Zeus made a decision to split them in half with his lightning. Like splitting a poached egg in half with a strand of hair, parting its pieces into two different locations. Their intentions accomplished, for now that we have been split we have lost our power. To work with another harmoniously has become a fictional tale. It is what everyone desires but has given up.

Our society then pressures us to share its own priorities, suppressing our ideals to search for that true love. Instead we are sucked into the capitalistic economy and we play out jobs, prioritising career, all the while forgetting life's true importance. To make up for the sorrow in our hearts, we settle. We make compromises against the self, in order to obtain company. We fill the abysmal void of our search with career and family, all the while forgetting (or trying to forget) the ideal life. That life that we truly desire now becomes the life that only took what it could get without disturbing its social responsibilities. Reproduction then creates the mediocre, and the divinity of what could of been is lost. The social inference of how to live life dominates, and creation becomes that of economic considerations. We act as sheep following the shepherds called the ways of society. Herd mentality follows the pointing fingers of whoever is in front of it.

What to search for? We are beings of biology. We are not given an instruction manual on how to live life. The question of what to look for in the soul mate lies within. One first needs to turn within before turning outside. To learn who it is that you are will give you an understanding of what you are looking for in another. To compromise is to go against the grain of who you are as a person. To trick yourself into believing that someone is your soul mate is the folly of so many of us. We are all on a journey, whether we realise it or not. To prematurely advance that journey will have its consequences. For it is courage that you need! Courage to stand through the trials and tribulations of loneliness and alienation, all the while observing the bigger picture. For it is the best possible life that you desire for yourself. To be beyond happy. To stand side by side with the one who is truly meant for you. To both "armour up" and battle each human condition in unison.

The lonely journey. This idea feels uneasy to us. One might feel as they are in a state of constant limbo. One's compatibility will be shown for what it is, and person after person will enter and leave their lives. Like seeing an enormous crowd, and shaking one's head at all. It will feel that what you desire is not out there, for it is an abyss. Life becomes a constant struggle directed towards finding something that appears to be nowhere. But one must realise what is at stake. For Arendt explains it well when she says, "it would be better for me that my lyre or a chorus I directed should be out of tune and loud with discord, and that multitudes of men should disagree with me rather than I, being one, should be out of harmony with myself and contradict me." (The Life of the Mind, p. 181) Our very being is on the line, and it is us that must suffer the consequences of our actions.

Faith as possibility. It becomes extremely tempting to give up this manhunt. When faced with the dark abyss of our odds, to continue the pursuit seems pointless. But if we give up, then what do our odds become? I have been told many times before to stop looking and the right person will come to me. I have thought about this statement a great deal and disagree with it. I guess that I could stop looking and the right person might come along and find me, but the chances of that are extremely slim. However, if I did not stop looking then I would still probably meet this person. If this one individual out there is looking as well, then our chances of finding each other increase. And I pray that this is the case. I hope that this one has not compromised and just obtained a someone, and I have faith that this is the case because I look at me and I have insight into that other. Like custom fit armour that has been tailored exactly to your body. For in faith, we bring possibilities. In spite of the absurd backfiring again and again, our hope must not dwindle, otherwise so do our possibilities. For when we act, we make tiny imprints on the universe. We leave bread crumbs specially tailored for that other to find us. By exercising our own faith (in all of its absurdity), we are directly and indirectly assisting our search for that special one that is out there. By putting ourselves out there again and again, our presence expands and we become more findable to that one.

The road. For it is about the journey. We must walk and walk. We are only ever given this moment, and this moment, and this moment. For it is this moment that we have and we must make use of. Along the way we will meet many interesting and wonderful people, many boring people, and many hurtful people. The lessons along the road will tell us where we should go and how we should be. In this journey we will find ourselves and become what we are. The path will give us insight into how we are to love all whom we encounter. It will show us how to treat each other and ourselves. To take each encounter as a wonderful gift that life has given to us is its results. We will learn how to appreciate people for what they give and who they are, and learn from them along the way. We will change the hearts of many and share our life lessons to those who have ears to hear.

Discipleship. Destined to be homeless, travelling from one place to another becomes tolerable. To exist as a wandering traveller searching for what is not seen. It was Jesus that said, "Foxes have holes and birds of the air have nests, but the Son of Man has no place to lay his head". (Matthew 8:20, NIV) One might enquire as to why I brought "religion" into it, but I did not. It was already there. We become warriors searching for the greatest love possible. Our search is a search for God. It is a search for the divinity of man to combine two of the like as one. To follow one's heart into the thick and thin is discipleship. Thus our journey is not a search for the One, but a search for the Divine, with its intended result being one's soul mate. It is a Holy journey that chases what is not seen, and that requires faith from the disciple.

Growth as a tool. And what are we to do with our time during this search? That one out there is someone incredibly special. In fact, the most special person in the world. Self development becomes our objective not only for ourselves but for that other. For when you finally do meet that other and give yourself over to them, you will be giving them a refined item. It is to give the Other the best You that you are able to give. The treasure of yourself, the self that you have built, becomes the most important gift that you could ever give. We make who we are in each "now" moment, and it is these "now" moments that must be utilised to achieve this refinement. It is the most special gift ever given, for it took your entire life to develop. It was built for that other and will mean the world to them, for it is a result of the search.

The Philosopher. Each becomes a philosopher, searching for wisdom, learning how to live the best life possible. The experiences that the world has gifted teach many lessons, and one learns well the differences between right and wrong. For along the road, one will see many hardships, both within social dysfunctions, families observed, and within the self. One will acquire the skills that they need to learn how to do the right thing in a diverse range of scenarios. One will be truly living life, refusing for it to live them. Society will act as an enemy, and at seemingly every direction one goes it will stand there shaking their heads. For its rules have been erased, and replaced with your own. For the seeker truly knows the folly's of society. It is for this reason that they will be able to help humanity more than anyone else.

Purity as proof. To demonstrate the seriousness of your dedication to the Other, one can choose the life of purity. To remove the possibilities of getting caught up with what one doesn't need, sexual abstinence offers a solution. It is in the material that we can get lost without perspective. To have control over that physical shows great passion and respect for the seriousness of the search and our ability to overcome our own urges. To rid oneself of the "list" that is made from sexual partner to sexual partner, and not fret over emotional attachments created as a result of those consequences. To live in purity becomes easy when the entire picture is seen in perspective. Every moment we are building towards some end or another. To build upon solid foundations with quality material is the best way to start a new relationship with that one when you find them. For they will be extremely appreciative for all of your efforts, to save yourself for specifically them. The gift of one's physical self will be seen as the greatest present to begin that divine relationship.

What of failure? What if the pursuer fails? This is the risk that they take. To strive for such an enormous task carries the possibility of failure. But let us look at it in perspective with the assumption of failure. To live this life is to live the best life that is possible. One will have acquired connections and friends wherever they have gone. One will be the best person that they can be and have led the best life that they could of lived, dedicated to the pursuit of their highest good. And how can you know unless you have tried? The possibilities do not arise unless they are strived for. I will not get fed unless food is acquired. The chances to become an actor do not manifest themselves until one acts. We do not live in a world where people stumble on opportunities all of the time, no matter how much movies or television shows tell us that we do. To see a return, one must enter. Our possibilities must be created.

The result - the product of a lifetime. And when we find that One our world changes. Two individuals with a similar purpose who would love to expand upon their own by acquiring the passions that the Other has that they do not yet possess. Four hands, two voices, and two well trained and conditioned minds who can take on the world together, not only loving each other, but also the world and the people in it - the best that they possibly can. Who not only put up with each other, but immerse themselves into the passion of their mirror. No longer confined by the limits that society places upon them, they are able to share a single life together. Vocation becomes their most passionate desires, and both are involved. Business as usual no longer confines them because they understand true value. Their lives will revolve around passion, compassion, self-improvement, and each other. Each will have a burning desire to show their lover how special they are, and will wish to make them as joyful as possible, while also encouraging equality and autonomy. For this is the divine result of the search. To be able to utilise two sets of hands in the poker game called life. Philosophy means nothing without the life backing up that meaning. This is the destiny for Seekers.

ACT 9
LEAP OF FAITH

Genesis 1:29-31
And God said, Behold, I have given you every herb bearing
seed, which is upon the face of all the earth, and every tree, in the
which is the fruit of a tree yielding seed; to you it shall be for meat.
And to every beast of the earth, and to every fowl of the air, and to
every thing that creepeth upon the earth, wherein there is life, I
have given every green herb for meat: and it was so. And God
saw every thing that he had made, and, behold, it was very good.
And the evening and the morning were the sixth day.

Sanity
There or Not?

Love is Not Its Contrary
25/06/2011

Love is a verb. Its meaning is lost without its expression. The actions behind the word constitutes its meaning. Lack thereof of its intended expression is directly in conflict with its meaning. To genuinely care for another and their interests stands as the beginning of the manifestation called 'love'. Anything in conflict with this premise is not a manifestation of love but of subjugation and oppression.

Each individual's search for love dominates their lives. The topic of concern for us all is what and who we love and how far that we will go to actualise our deepest desires. Those desires are what makes each and every one of us special - an individual. For any other to ignore those desires and replace them with their own expedient purposes, meaning looking at their own ends and not another's means, is directly in conflict with love.

Throughout the development of the historical existence of the human race, we have learnt time and time again that a tyrannical system is not only doomed to failure but also an incredibly unjust and invasive form of government. For the interests of another to be given to them by another, in turn suppressing the other's sense of values, motivations, desires, wishes, and self worth results in a caste system where the life of one individual is worth more than the life of another individual.

To elaborate on this subject, the lives of those who follow the path that the media lays for them results in the working class. To create the media that is followed by others spawns the ruling class. To do neither is to be labelled as 'an undesirable' who is incapable of 'making decisions'. This is a system put in place to clear the bowling lane of left over pins and then [re-processing] them.

Just as with any system of rules and regulations, there will be a certain amount of individuals who cannot comply within its borders. Values will not always sufficiently be passed down and a portion of the population will suffer extreme forms of disapproval and alienation. Where the individual falls short to conform to the pressures of society is where the individual is told again and again that it is THEIR problem. A healthy individual with different values than that of cultural normality is looked down upon and declared unhealthy. The idea of freedom becomes absurd and all that is presented is a few options, ultimately giving ultimatums if one does not comply, independent if one is or is not a danger to themselves or others.

Welcome to tyrannical conditioning. A system developed and enforced to collect and [re-process] the 'undesirables'. Now that you are here, YOU are the subject of inquiry. Your limits will be tested, overstepped, broken, and then shredded. You are no longer considered a human being but a lesser mammal. Your wants and desires are no longer considered but what they system wants for you is now your new life. Non-compliance is futile. Resistance is futile. The system has all the time in the world to batter you until compliance occurs. If you think yourself to have hope, the system will take it away.

To go against the grain of love is not love. To intentionally leave out ones goals, interests, objectives, personality, ambitions, and desires is not love but intentional and volitional malice. I pray for the souls of every individual involved in this terrible process. Many believe their deeds to be helping. I assert that this place can rarely 'help' a person. Welcome to Hell. I have heard that one never 'truly' leaves.

Everchanging Values
02/07/2011
Written to the conglomerate of an insane asylum.

I once valued similar things to all of you. I owned cars, a home, had family, cared about money, cared about accommodation, desired to own possessions, and lived day to day in a world that most would consider reasonably "normal". But two things changed all of that. 1) Living life, and 2) Learning.

Many things that I once valued in my life were suddenly taken away. This then allowed me to evaluate what it really was that I truly valued and many of those things were superficial and became devalued or even worthless. I have experienced much in my life, and I felt it all. I felt my way through life. I also felt my way through learning, for example, my search for knowledge. I did not "pick up" philosophy, but FELT through it, therefore its ramifications fell on me like the unstable brick wall that life is.

I now sit here imprisoned by the same government that I swore my allegiance to. I am too different for any to understand, so I am treated as a mentally insane patient. I know the taboo of that word, but you cannot just rename the word to make your connotations different. Because my values do not reflect those of your own society and culture, I have become a project to prod at to see my reaction. The majority of my freedoms have been stripped from me, and once again, my values are shifting. And this time, the needle, the catalyst, is you.

Before I was imprisoned here I used to value many things. I used to value Internet access and freedom of information. I have little concern about that now. I used to value keeping in contact with those on the Internet. I no longer care. I used to value freedom and democracy as one of my highest goods. I now know no such thing to exist. I once valued a caring government but that does not exist either.

You have chipped away at me and now I am a product of your oppression. My mind has transcended the physical and I no longer hold any values within its realm. The only thing that I care about now is my morals and the way that I choose to live my life. I will never fall out of sync with myself. It is better to be out of sync with the entire world than myself. You can take me out of sync with absolutely everything in your control, but you will never achieve your objective. I am not an "episode" and am actually insulted that you consider my personality as such. You can feed my body, starve my mind, and try and tear away at my soul, but my soul is strong and you are in a losing battle, no matter how much or what methods you try.

To take an entirely free bird from its home and sticking it in a box is your crime. The only difference is that I am human.

However, I am not one to ignore the positive. I came in here because I was struggling with my ego desiring what it did not have. I have suffered much in my life because I was not content with what was and thought that it should be better. Thanks to your unruly procedures, my ego has receded to what its function is: to take care of one's functional needs and nothing more. I am no longer suicidal because my ego is deflated. My ego is where I want it; the reason I came into this mouse trap. I appreciate your oppression to teach me what I needed to learn.

But there comes a point where one must ask how much longer they will endure torture. I was told by another that psychiatrist take an oath to "do no harm". If this is true, mine is breaking theirs. Please remove my shackles so that I can get external help to reverse some of the damage you have inflicted.

05/07/2011

My freedom is taken away like it was never there nor important. I am then treated on and not with. My desired teamwork faded away and I became the rat in a cage, without a say or a soul. No matter the amount of research or standing up for my rights I perform, my cries remain ignored because I have become less than human. My dream of traveling around Australia as a student seems to dwindle away. I have come to understand freedom for its true colors: non-existent. I can not be the person that my psychiatrist wants me to be because my personality is not a psychotic episode or results thereof.

All expect me to be calm. To sugar coat the truth to make everybody happy. My feelings have become irrelevant in a system that has stripped my freedom: oppresses and subjugates me on a day to day basis. My interests have been tossed aside like yesterday's paper and externally created interests put in its place. My search to not become a number has proved absurd and a number is all that I am. To be "normal" is my oppressors objective, but I cannot comply. I have been told that if one complies when I am deployed back into society and revert back to non-compliance, that one will end up back here. I have been told by those who have experienced this. I am discredited and those who care can do nothing.

- Why can't we all just get along?
- Why are so many's actions deviant?
- Why do so many ignore the golden rule?
- Why do we oppress those who care and accept those who are malicious?
- Why do I see extremely violent individuals come and leave, and my non-aggressive self, stays right here?
- Why does the system not work with individuals but instead against them?
- Why do professionals believe that they are always in the right?
- Why must people lie?
- Why is volitional malice commonplace?
- Why can a Westerner not be a monk?
- What did I do wrong?
- Why is it wrong to be myself?
- Why has God forsaken me?
- Why am I here? What is its meaning?
I Love Myself

Tears roll down my face like boulders rolling down a hill as I ponder the reality of my situation. Two weeks and a few days has thus far been my sentence at the Ballarat Acute Psychiatric Facility. I have been informed that I suffer from a "thought illness". The lifetime that it took me to condition my mind the way that I desired it has been spit all over, and my views and interpretations that I have found as a result of my life's studies is belittled as the result of a psychotic illness.

My life's search for meaning and greater understanding is not "normal" thus needs treating. The fact that I never attempted to be "normal" remains unconsidered, and I get stuck in a system attempting to "normalise" me. The fact that my life has been spent to remove the box and not think inside it remains ignored. Their objective: to make me "normal". To revert the mental conditioning that I have spent my life project moulding. My moral development as an individualist is assessed as inappropriate and a more collective set of moral guidelines handed to me offered as the only route to freedom. What is continually ignored is that I love myself! I love my brain, my ideas, my creativity, and my courage.

I have spent my life breaking outside of the box for a reason: because I did not like what was inside the box. It held nothing but hostility and empty promises. It gave ignorance and consumerism as its gifts and I saw those not to be gifts but instead bait. Bait to get sucked into an meaningless life. A life without meaning but instead systems that were put in place to keep the power and control in the hands of the greedy, in turn allowing the caste system to exist, dividing a planet that naturally is undivided.

I hate currency. Others attempt to push me to say that it is fine for some people but I no longer think that it is. To use currency beyond basic needs is to agree that there is value in said plastic. It is to agree to work with a system that will only work with you if you conform to its values. It encourages greed and creates an "economy" that apparently "runs the world". But it does not. This life is not about money but the people around you. Money becomes a worshipped idol when one cannot live without it. When money directs one's every move in life, money has broken an ethical barrier and becomes a source of great evil. Our society is run by a great source of evil, and it resides in our pockets. And it is precisely views like this that stand as the reason I am in this insane asylum. I have been declared an untouchable by society - incompatible with your system.

But the fact that I love myself, or better stated, the person that I have built myself to be, remains an ignored factor. The reason I am imprisoned here is not because of my own dealings with myself, but my dealings with society. The object of my conditioning has been declared unfit for the general public. I am being [re-processed] because I am now, like my philosophical investigation into reality, consciousness, sentience, and subjective interpretation, am ethereal. I am the fog of war and my captivity is the attempt to clear the ground. All expect to understand by direct language but that is impossible. I use my words to paint a picture. I realise these words to be unsatisfactory to convey real meaning, so I utilise them to strive for the conveyance of a more abstract but at the same time more articulate meaning. I can never express what it is that I am trying to express but I can make a painting to get as close to there as I can. My words are the results of my paint brush called my mouth or pen. I have absolutely no problems with my thinking. I have spent my life refining and fine tuning it. Do not punish me just because I do not fit your ideal. I fit exactly my ideal. I am a philosopher and it is the philosopher's job to remove all preconceptions. Do not punish me for what I am. I am not hurting anyone. In fact, just the opposite. I strive for love every conscious second. This is the God that I worship.

Parental Complex
09/07/2011

A few days after I entered this psychiatric ward I fasted for three days. I found out, as a result of the fast, that I am never content with [what is], which causes me to excessively strive for something that [is not]. I have used my life always pushing for what could be and not what was. This was the cause of my suffering: I am learning to be content with what is.

In light of this information, I believe that I have found the root of this deeply seeded striving and it lies as a result from my parents. They are the ones that have never been happy with me - my decisions in life and the person that I choose to be. I cannot remember the last time I talked to either of my parents and them actually display happiness for my choices that I made in life. The more I learn and the more I become, the more my parentals display their disapproval. They are never happy or content with [what is] in my life, but always critical, pushing for [what is not].

I believe that this constant disapproval in my life helped fashion me. I kept learning how to be better, but it was never in line with what either of my parents thought to be better. My parents constant push for me to change, constantly pushed me to change, but not in the direction they hoped for.

I believe my father has stopped doing this recently. I think that he has "given up", but in fact this could be beneficial for our relationship. At first I thought him to no longer care, but after some time I have found him standing back to be beneficial to our future relationship. He no longer seems to make judgements about any of my life. Maybe eventually we can reconcile our relationship and some day he might be happy for my person. But I will be content with [what is] and not grasp at the wind.

My mother on the other hand is just as hard headed as I am. She believes that she has been enlightened with all the answers. And her answer: "do not think". She wants what she thinks is best for me. And what she thinks is best for me is for me to not be me. And I believe it better to be out of sync with the entire world than with myself. It is easy to see the direct conflict that my mother and I desire in my future. The bulls butt heads. She desires so much for me to not be me that she will spend passionate effort expressing to me that she knows how my life should go and it is not how I currently choose to live it. She will go out of her way to make her disapproval known to me. She feels as if I am her responsibility even though I have not been her responsibility since 1999. She is never happy with [what is] and always strives for me to be [what is not]. This is my inherited suffering. These are my tears in life. Because I am never "right" in her eyes, or my own.

Community is Belonging
18/07/2011
A writing contest for an insane asylum that was refused entry.

To belong is to be comfortable within one's environment. Humans are communal creatures who excel within social environments. To belong is to know and love oneself, sharing one's talents and gifts with all who are around that can benefit from them. To belong one must find themselves and then figure out how their gifts and talents can be used to benefit others around them.

In order to be good for others, one must first be good for themselves. Before others can reap the benefits of one's offerings, one first needs a healthy mind and a healthy body. Without a healthy mind, the body will not know how to coherently interact with its surroundings. Similarly, without a healthy body, the mind cannot optimise its pathway. To belong one must first themselves reach a healthy status to be any good for others.

Once mental and physical health is obtained, one stands in a lighthouse, able to see clearly what it is that is around them and what direction they need to go. With health comes the ability to make clear and concise decisions directed towards the future. When physical and mental health is obtained, one is able to objectively assess their own ability and figure out one's place within the community where they belong and not where other people tell them that they belong.

Being is belonging. But sometimes our minds are too busy from distractions of our own lives to see what being really is. Being is observed as our day to day struggles but this could not be further from the truth of being. To 'be' consists of a conscious awareness.

This awareness does not necessarily need any external factors upon it to be. Being can be awakened when one just sits and recognises what it is; what they are. Not what happened in their lives or what they are diagnosed with, but instead a conscious perception that sees over those things. One's being necessitates one's belonging. To belong one has to be. And for one to be, one can choose to be aware of their beingness or not. But if we choose to recognise this being, it will make it clear to us that we are not our diagnosis nor our history. All we have in this life is the now and we choose how we live it every second. To live it in the moment, ensuring our mental and physical health, will give us the most optimal life that we can live every second along the way.

To be is belonging. Belonging is communal. Just as the right hand becomes incoherent without the left, our mission in life is to find out what body part we are and learn to function as it the best we can. To belong in a community is not conforming with what said community wants you to be, but being yourself to the best of your ability.

Hospital Feedback
01/08/2011

To the insane asylum quality control,

I have been shaped and moulded by your counterparts to be a submissive collectivist who conforms to whatever it is that his superiors wishes upon him. I was once an individual who took pride in being something different, but now have been punished for this mentality. The only way that I found to be released from your prison that you call a hospital, was to shake my head and agree with whatever it was that was being pushed upon me. My beliefs were demeaned as a product of a mental illness, and my character was run over again and again by your hooligans that you call mental health professionals. My concerns were not taken into consideration, but instead a new set of concerns were given to me by these "professionals". A hospital that is full of mentally unsound people does not even have a counsellor available to speak to, when most people really need to speak to someone who could help them talk out their minds. The psychiatrists stood as an enemy to all patients. There is good reason for this. Because they are not concerned about the well being of their patient but only what their next action towards the patient will be. Their lack of empathy comes across to the patients as cruelty, and instead of creating a "win-win" situation, you have created "us and them".

Complete and utter compliance is your health professional's goal. They not only push one to agree with the given diagnosis, but also push one to agree with their chosen treatment path, which does not involve one's input. I noticed both in myself and in other people around me that there existed a general consensus with what the doctors wanted to hear, and as long as you responded in this manner, the professionals would loosen their grips on you. My suspicions were verified after I started conforming, shaking my head to whatever treatment that was forced upon me. It was at that point that I began to acquire leave. Your tight grip loosens whenever conformity is achieved. And conformity is the only option that you give. One can forget about working with the staff to achieve an optimal treatment plan that is best for you. One is given a method that is solidly created by your professionals that is apparently best for you. Any negotiation of this plan is seen as non-compliance and is dealt with by the tightening grips of your system's cold fingers. To work with your system is impossible. Your system does not make way for one to work with it. You create the "us and them" mentality, and wonder why your patients receive a poor taste in their mouths. The psychiatrist waves their brutal sword called a pen and condemns their plan on you, to be carried out by the nurses using whatever means necessary. The psychiatrist does not have the patient's health in mind, but their compliance. All is well as long as the patient has no will of their own.

The ward is not a place of healing but instead a place of misery. Healing is not encouraged. Not a soul responds to one's tears. The ward is reduced as a holding cell to ensure that patients consume their medications. The consistent malice from other patients confirms this premise. You have not provided a very nice atmosphere to encourage healing, nor are the staff trained to be effective counsellors to anyone. One must ask the same question many times to a staff member to get an appropriate response. Every time one request something from a staff member they cross their fingers hoping the patient forgets. This becomes extremely irritating and makes the patient feel as if they are bothering the staff member for them to merely do their job.

This has been the worst thing that I have ever experienced in my life. The psychiatrist is not concerned with my life and the way that I wish to live it, but a statistical life and the way that it generally lives it. Your unit does not provide a holistic healing environment but instead a prison to "re-process" people you deem as mentally unsound in society – people who do not pass your bar of sanity. Your process was quick to deem my personality traits which I have intentionally built over many years as schizophrenic psychotic episodes or results thereof. The psychiatrists' agenda is to compartmentalise an individual. To place an individual into a box and make them a statistic so they can treat them with more statistics. To have my spiritual and philosophical understandings entirely undermined and written off was extremely insulting. To compartmentalise my found understandings as by-products of a mental illness was out of line.

I was told by my psychiatrist that "I lack insight into my condition", but this was the end of the conversation and not the beginning. To be disillusioned means that sight is not clear. I was not told where my sight was unclear. The beginning of a conversation was pushed

39

as the end. Was I supposed to just blindly accept that I was wallowing in misunderstandings and leave it at that? You raise a huge point of concern and try to package it up as the illness. "You have a thought illness called Schizophrenia, which causes you to be disillusioned. That is all, next." I think that you all have a thought disorder for expecting me to blindly accept your conclusions without leading me to real conclusions – to find out what it is that we are speaking about so that we can truly treat it. But it is not the goal of your system to treat the root cause, but instead treat symptoms. Well I do not work that way, unless of course all of my freedom is stripped from me and I am reduced to an insane patient who does not know what is good for himself. Then I will work whatever way that you tell me to, because that is how you loosen your grips.

If it was under my control I would investigate down the line to find the root cause of my problems, so then I could work on that instead of just treating symptom after symptom. Your system will never truly help people because it ignores the root cause! Otherwise you would at least have psychologist readily available to speak to those who need to speak to someone. Nurses are not sufficient as qualified psychologist. Attempting to push this role on to them is out of line. And most do not have the time of day for their patients. Patients need someone who wants to speak to them. Who cares about them and their feelings. Who wants to help them help themselves. A caring listening ear who is trained to help patients sort out their own thoughts is one of the many things that you guys do not provide.

How is one supposed to remedy lack of insight? By carefully studying that which we are talking about. My "mental illness", my medications, my lost perceptions, related conditions, brain chemistry, and any other related scientific understandings of my said delusions. But this was impossible seeing as there was no material related to this. I had to push hard for the Wikipedia's that I did get. There was no studying what it was the doctors were telling me. Only blind acceptance, which is what you pushed every second of the way. Blind compliance was your agenda. That is the cookie cutter mould for all of your patients. Don't let them think for themselves, we will think for them.

I am told that I am disillusioned for burning my identification. I am not. I saw a problem – the root of the problem – and did what I needed to do to begin its rectification. Those numbers all over everything that apparently is, "me", are in fact not me. I have been reduced to a number my entire life. Your system reduces each individual to a number – a statistic that can be treated by other statistics. You have forgotten that there are real people behind these faces. The faces to you are only mentally insane patients who are grouped by their diagnosis. Surprise! Your diagnosis is not that person. You try to persuade each individual to agree with their diagnosis so that they too can compartmentalise themselves into a box and agree with your treatment plan, a treatment plan that can fit your subjective ideas on how a person should live their life and how they should be. Individualism is thrown out the door and replaced with collectivism, whether one likes it or not. Your ideals become the only ideal and the only option is to conform. You think you are helping? You need to reflect whether you are really helping. And if your answer is, "Yes, I am helping", my question to you is, "By whose standards?".

Once admitted in your hospital, one cannot win. One must be extremely careful of their language because it will be taken out of context and used against you at a later date. One is damned if they speak and damned if they do not. At one point I chose to exercise my freedom of silence and a senior staff member responded extremely inappropriately, for example, "grow up", "act your age", "stop being a child". If one speaks, at a later date your words will be taken out of its context to develop a case against you. If you do not speak, that too will develop a case against you. Once in your system, one cannot win. You are already insane. You are damned by your policies and procedures, and everything will be done to not only try and disprove your sanity, but also get you to question whether you have indeed lost your sanity. Everything you once valued is questioned and deemed the manifestations of a madman. Your system is insane. It needs to go through your system so it can be judged by itself. Only then can it understand how evil it is.

How has your system helped me? It has not. I could not voice my concerns because if I did I would of remained captive in your system for much longer. Now that I am out I plan to get my medication right [off] and get better. Your detention centre does not give room for one to get better. Locking one up against their will - stripping them from all their freedom and treating them as mad when they have done nothing wrong does not help. The only improvements that occurred during my unwilling stay in your prison was done from me. I was able to work on myself. Now is my time to reverse the damage that you have done to me. Now that I am out, treatment is on my terms. I will get help while learning so that I can make up my own mind about what is happening to me and what I want to happen to me. Like I said to begin with, I know myself better than any of you because I spent my life learning myself. I was the best man for the job but you bypassed that man. Now that man is back and he will chase treatment that works for him instead of you. You should of just kept me apart of my treatment to begin with. That was all I asked for.

Sincerely,

Wendell

I do not stop writing these people.

They ignore me.

ACT 10
LOVE'S FREEDOM
May 9, 2011

When we stand back and observe romantic relationships within our own cultural enframement we are led to ask why suffering is so tightly wound up with our conception and application of love. Let us journey together through the abstract nature of love to extract true value.

Introduction. Our love stands strong as a guide to the decisions that one chooses on a day to day basis. One's time is directed towards increasing happiness by seeking that which is loved. Unfortunately, the uninvited guest named 'suffering' seems to present itself the closer that we get to reaching this love. Are we merely captives to current conceptions of love? For love to merely exist to encourage reproduction seems to discredit the importance of this love. To label one's love as an inevitable conflict between individuals exposes love as hopeless. There appears to be something hidden in the very concept of love that could stand as knowledge itself. But to access this knowledge, must one necessarily suffer? It could stand to reason that suffering is a result of the corruption of love and does not manifest from love itself.

Love's Ideological Captivity. At birth, an infant is passed an ideological preconception of their purpose. A cookie cutter that was also passed to the infants caretaker. A purpose to find

43

happiness through romantic love. Current culture hands the cookie cutter to the infant and expects it to readily jump into the cutter's borders. The infant is expected to grow within that cookie cutter so that eventually they can be what current culture expects it to be. If one decides not to use that cookie cutter to mould their being, they become something not understood. They become alienated by those whom are different from their own culturally relative collective teachings.

The present ideological cookie cutter within Western culture pressures each individual to value romantic love as ultimate life purpose. One is held captive to a particular ideology of love. Romantic love is obsessed over, which causes great anguish on the subjects psychology. For one to have a 'good' life, one is expected to grow up, fall in love, have a family, work, retire, and then die. How is one to react to this ideology of love? It appears premature to assert that romantic love will achieve this happiness when relationship after relationship struggles and falls apart in front of our eyes. Culture's notion of 'love' seems to cause its people great amounts of pain and suffering. To say that romantic love can truly lead us to personal happiness seems extremely rash when one can understand from the observations in their own lives, countless unhealthy, miserable, and failed romantic partnerships.

Defining an Abstract such as 'Love'. To define romantic love, the haze of the abstraction must be cleared. It seems to manifest in each individual and guide their entire lives. One is led to investigate culture and what purpose it serves and why it is so highly valued in our current society. The ability to achieve happiness appears to be very closely tied to love. When we attempt to define this love, we tend to only be able to define what it is not, which creates confusion by comparison. This ultimately steers us away from our subjects real essence, which is and can only be itself.

According to Schopenhauer, one's desire for romantic love is heavily dependant on the human desire to reproduce for the greater good of the species from an impersonal level. To reproduce is to continue one's own self. It is to continue ones own existence in and through another. He asserts,

"he will specially desire in the other individual those perfections that he himself lacks; in fact, he will even find beautiful those imperfections that are the opposite of his own. Hence, for example, short men look for tall women, persons with fair hair like those with dark, and so on. The delusive ecstasy that seizes a man at the sight of a woman whose beauty is suited to him, and pictures to him a union with her as the highest good, is just the sense of the species." Schopenhauer continues, "Therefore, what here guides man is really an instinct directed to what is best for the species, whereas man himself imagines he is seeking merely a heightening of his own pleasure." (Arthur Schopenhauer, The World As Will and Representation (New York: Dover, 1958), 539)

From this heteronormative perspective, one can understand romantic love to exist like a magic trick presented to the audience. Each individual is asked, "Is this your card?", and the responses are, "Wow, yes!". However, the factual trick is that all of the cards are the same. One believes this magic trick to be performed specific to their own individual selves, when in actual fact, they are simply the subjects of nature's own agenda: to sexually reproduce to improve the genetic gene pool of future generations.

The accuracy of this depiction does not account for many types of relationships. Homosexual, asexual, virus infected, and infertile relationships present an innate flaw in Schopenhauer's conclusion. In current society, one does not always seek what one lacks within the other, and one might seek similarities rather than genetic development. Short people might seek short people, and tall people might seek tall people. It could stand to reason that Schopenhauer's depiction was composed of his own cultural cookie cutter, that encouraged a cleaner genetic pool.

We are left with something hidden that is difficult to pinpoint or even articulate. The cookie cutter has given the mould, but not explained the reason why this particular mould should be utilized instead of another.

The Experiment. Upon commencing my investigations into this topic, I was asked by a co-worker, "What? You don't already understand what love is?" I responded with, "No, do you?" He brushed me off pridefully stating, "You must be stupid." I questioned him seeking his declared wisdom asking, "What do you know love to be?" His initial reply consisted of multiple linguistic filler words, followed with, "I can't believe that you don't know what love is."

The more I learn about this topic, the more I understand its unchecked ramifications. Just as Aristotle teaches one to practically integrate wisdom from thoughts into actions (Aristotle, Nicomachean Ethics, translated by W. D. Ross (ebook, 1994), 4), my mission became to find out how others around me understood and interpreted this subject. It was at this point I commenced an experiment. One individual after another I sat down with, in attempts to extract a more competent understanding of my current cultures understanding of love, asking the popular but seemingly unanswered question, "What is love?"

I asked this question to a large number of age groups, sexual orientations, and relationship statuses. I spoke with over thirty individuals. In every case, the trend of hesitance and surprise carried on from the original subject. I was able to extract little to no information from a single person. Most concluded that I was mentally inept for asking such an 'obvious' question. From one perspective, the experiment was a failure. But was it really? This tells me that there is definitely something hiding in love. Something that others feel more comfortable to act within instead of articulating. The blurry heart now stands out as being what it is: extremely blurry. In a love driven society, we seem to know very little about it. Could suffering contribute to our cultural naivety on the topic of "love"?

Consideration also must be given to the cultural confinement of this experiment. This only accounts for a small portion of individuals whom reside and have contact with me within the small military town of Augusta, Georgia, USA. This experiment might assist us in our investigations, but can in no way account for the entire world or even all of Augusta. Our topic of love remains a mystery, and reasons why one would choose to endure through its suffering remains an abstraction. However, if our position shifts to observe another side of the metaphorical cube in question, answers may follow.

Conflict! It stands to question whether the source of this desired happiness is misplaced. To identify personal happiness primarily within another directly puts us eye to eye with the bull. Sartre asserts that a relationship places us in direct conflict with the other.

"While I attempt to free myself from the hold of the Other, the Other is trying to free himself from mine; while I seek to enslave the Other, the Other seeks to enslave me."(Jean-Paul Sartre, Being and Nothingness (New York: Washington Square Press, 1961), 77)

From this perspective, ones task is to claim a type of ownership of the other. A role to capture the freedom of the other. It is not a 'love potion' that is desired, but a free choice to give up some of thyself for the other and the likewise, directed towards one's own person. Both parties desire for the other to utilize their freedom to in turn suppress their autonomy to comply with the asserted requirements of the other. To freely and passionately commit oneself to that other, but ironically, resulting in destruction of parts of that very freedom in question. Thus, for Sartre, a direct conflict exists between both parties who desire to own the current object of their affection. Both parties actively and constantly winning and losing parts of themselves within their expectations and requirements of and from the other. It lies unconsciously as the goal of each involved to strive to recover those parts of themselves that have been lost as a result of the other's subjugation.

I for one do not wish to be the cause of a process as sinister as this. To gain an ability to effectively fix mechanical problems, one must understand the mechanical problems involved. To be able to relate this depiction in almost every relationship that I have seen frightens me. But this is not written in stone and I cannot accept this to always be the case. Two individuals aware of these mechanical workings will be equipped with tools that many are not. They do not have to be doomed to this fate.

True Hidden Knowledge. Reflecting on the prior survey, we are led to interrogate what love really is and how it functions. The hidden seems special. For Nussbaum, the not so obvious is in fact just the opposite: the only given. This given seems to not just be an abstract concept, but true knowledge itself. As science acts as a vehicle directed towards knowledge, love stands as the knowledge itself. This love that we are very careful before verbalization, but drives our entire life, acting not just as a word, but stands as true knowledge itself.

"knowledge of our love is not the fruit of the impression of suffering, a fruit that might in principle have been apart from suffering. The suffering itself is a piece of self-knowing." (Martha C. Nussbaum, Loves Knowledge (New York: Oxford, 1990), 267)

This places perspective on our topic's experiment. To articulate love is to place the known into the less known. The vehicle to communicate this knowledge might lie within intellectual scrutiny, however, in doing this, the result is only backtracking from the known. From this knowledge that we truly know stands impossible to reject. It is already known, felt, and acted within. It is there and is contradictory to what one already knows to proclaim any different.

Love's Anguish. How can one come to understand and cope with all the pain and suffering that manifests as a result of our love? The moment the other departs one's side, suffering incurs. To love one is required to make sacrifices that demean their own individual autonomy. It is to place trust in a fallible being to continue to carry out this role. To love is to take many risks, some that could result in human suffering. Each heart knows this, yet most persist in a constant struggle directed towards love. If Nussbaum is correct, love is not something that can be avoided because it already is. Each individual is guided by it. To avoid it is to avoid true knowledge itself. It is what it is, and the knowledge it manifests as a result is observed in the actions of every individual.

The relevant inquiry seems not to be, "What is?", but instead, "What can one do about it?" For Nussbaum, the answer lies in learning how to fall. (Martha C.Nussbaum, Loves Knowledge (New York: Oxford, 1990), 274 - 280) As within martial arts, to avoid intense pain and suffering, one must learn how to fall. To reduce the great suffering that is involved with falling, one can learn how to fall so that minimal damage is inflicted. Suffering can exist as a learning utility to avoid future critical wounds. If thrown to the ground by another, one can learn to sit back into the force of the fall and prepare for the impact. The result is still the ground, but the damage inflicted is minimized. To rise up, brush oneself off, and move on can become an inconvenience which does not need to cripple us.

Why Suffer? Learning how to fall appears to be a great deal more appealing than ignorant suffering. Can it stand as a solution to assist humankind to deal with the pain and suffering that love brings about? Are we still missing something? Falling still entails suffering of some sort. Humans do not wish to suffer. Can suffering from the human heart be strained and removed instead of merely creating new and inventive coping mechanisms? Without suffering, all that is left is joy. Is this not what we are all striving for? Tolle suggests that we can indeed remove suffering from our lives, and the culprit of suffering lies in human selfishness.

"Humanity is destined to go beyond suffering, but not in the way the ego thinks. One of the ego's many erroneous assumptions, one of its many deluded thoughts is "I should not have to suffer." Sometimes the thought gets transferred to someone close to you: "My child should not have to suffer." That thought itself lies at the root of suffering. Suffering has a noble purpose: the evolution of consciousness and the burning up of the ego. The man on the Cross is an archetypal image. He is every man and every woman. As long as you resist suffering, it is a slow process because the resistance creates more ego to burn up. When you accept suffering, however, there is an acceleration of that process which is brought about by the fact that you suffer consciously. You can accept suffering for yourself, or you can accept it for someone else, such as your child or parent. In the midst of conscious suffering, there is already the transmutation. The fire of suffering becomes the light of consciousness." (Eckhart Tolle, A New Earth (New York: Penguin Group, 2008), 64)

Without the expectations that one should not need to suffer, suffering becomes absurd and its very definition collapses. If suffering is humbly accepted the process to remove suffering begins. By no longer identifying with the causes of suffering, the human being in turn transcends it. To reposition ones perspective on expectation is to entirely change the situation. Without suffering, all that is left is joy. The remnants is pure love. Love that can stand strong without lust, gluttony, greed, sloth, wrath, envy, or pride. To truly love another is to toss out the cookie cutter entirely and reinstate it, not with a cooking utensil, but itself. It is erroneous attempts to define such an amazing word as "love" using comparisons of what it is not will fail. But when we look at what it is, our perception is transmuted from what current culture tells it to be, and what it really is.

Conclusion. To love without the demon of suffering waiting around the corner can enlighten our perspective on how one chooses to pursue their love. To love virtuously, independent of its corruptions, can be to recognize the cultural conflict that Sartre raises, learn from its ramifications as Nussbaum asserted, and accept it in its entirety as Tolle suggests. For one to love does not also necessitate that one must suffer. Suffering, however, does serve a righteous purpose: its own destruction. Suffering is not a welcome emotion and most healthy individuals will do what they can to avoid it. It appears that the best way to avoid it might just be to embrace it. To remove love of its suffering can enable one to share a purer form of love with their special someone. Love itself.

Bibliography

Schopenhauer, Arthur, The World as Will and Representation, translated by E.F.J. Payne (New York: Dover, 1958)
Aristotle, Nicomachean Ethics, translated by W. D. Ross (1994)
Sartre, Jean-Paul, Being and Nothingness, translated by Hazel E. Barnes (New York: Washington Square Press, 1961)
Nussbaum, Martha C, Love's Knowledge: Essays on Philosophy and Literature (New York: Oxford, 1990)
Tolle, Eckhart, A New Earth (New York: Penguin Group, 2008)

A university assignment that I put my entire heart into and only obtained a Credit for. Why? Our current education system does not need to justify itself.

ACT 11
THE MARK OF HUMANITY
February, 2012

Throughout our ancient history, ideals were passed through the generations through the use of tablets, parchments, and the like. The invention of the printing press caused a huge intellectual boom in which new conceptions of everything arose. The creation of the Internet has opened up a door for a new golden age if we only play our cards right...

In the beginning God brought about all things and cast a conscious self awareness within Adam and Eve, and it was good. God was made known to them through their environment, for they saw that all the individual details acted as representations of their origin. As the ideal couple develops through the joys of life, they become enticed by the conception of existing in the same nature as God. They examined their psychology and made the necessary arrangements in order to achieve this divine nature. Ignorant to them was the ramifications of their actions. The causal chain fell upon them and they became naked.

God had given humans everything they wanted, including the ability to become it, that is to live in its nature. The hardships of the struggle to actualise god-like characteristics overwhelmed the newly formed self-awareness. Thus it became a struggle to align themselves with the psychology in which they modified. The growing burdens of the world crashes down upon them and they die. History has lived the consequences of their choices, and we will soon not forget the virtues of their actions. For they paved the way for human kind to take our place on the throne, as the demigod's that we are. And if our follies destroy us before we get there, then humankind would of proven its unworthiness for its bestowed honour.

As the original man had not the facilities for understanding, they employed the use of tools in their strife towards the divine. They learned to effectively communicate with each other and their environment. They learned to create methods for conveying meaning by utilising the planet's resources. Ideals passed through the generations and the one's with solid foundations outlasted any sword. Ideals are passed by written communication through a medium such as scrolls, animal skins, tablets, and the like. These ideals were preserved but exclusively available to the educated, wealthy, and powerful. The printing press is then invented and the scope of education spectrums. We then develop wonderful new technology as a result of these methods of media distribution. The golden age results from a careful analysis of our psychology in an attempt to articulate the abstraction.

Computers are born and act as a basic representation of its human creator. Human memory looks into the mirror and electronic storage is discovered. The technology develops and copulas amounts of information becomes portable. These computers naturally evolve to become like their Creator and network themselves together. This then brings about computer networking data centres that enable any desired resource to be at every humans fingertips with the use of any portable or fixed communication device.

The toils of Adam and Eve and their descendants is near its realisation. The history of man had to actualise itself through a long process of suffering. It had to overcome its physical and mental hardships. It had to create the required technology to effectively retrain its own psychology towards healthy methods of mental distribution.

We are so close to being free from our chains! The Internet unlocks our shackles and manifests a moral responsibility on everyone. The path of ignorance will show itself for its superfluous qualities, and one will be in common understanding to realise that the reason for all errors in judgement is only a result of a learning process or sheer laziness to educate oneself. No longer will the government rule our education and we the people will teach each other!

When vast ranges of University grade educations are obtainable through easy, popular, and free methods of distribution over the Internet, the seekers of the world have the necessary means to achieve an infinite spectrum of potential. When one is given a mind to fill which has no observable limits, the blank slate is transformed into a life sculpture. The potential individuality of the creator that creates their own mind has the potential to achieve god-like characteristics. The day will come upon us when the merit of each individual is no longer assessed by their status in society, currency in their bank, or qualifications accumulated but instead through the character and abilities in which they possess. When we form ourselves into what we are from ourselves as a result of the external in which guides our passions, we align ourselves with God. And from the creations of mankind will come great things that represent our divine image.

With such power comes great responsibility, and we must carefully consider how such involvements could result. We are nearing the end of our poisoned fruit and the future of our races quality and longevity will come into question. The collective result of our answers to our problems will determine the possibility of continued existence. Judgement day will come upon us and we will have to pay for the consequences of our actions. Evolution will enquire into our overall well-being and we must answer honestly. When the search for knowledge is at everyone's fingertips, we possess no excuses.

The turn from the phenomena of the world into the psychology of the sufferer has given our kind the tools to overcome our mundane. Asceticism has crafted mankind an adaptable mould to go beyond their physical and mental limitations. When we prepare the body and mind for any conditions, the mind lets go of needing anything. And when the finer things in life make their way to us, those things are realised and appreciated for their true value. The continual need for this and that keeps us shackled to our turmoil. Thus, to live in the moment without any needs opens up the true scope of our freedom and we escape our constant clinging. When we come to understand suffering as the wise teacher that it is, our disdain for it will fade into the background. For this or that pain is only an experience and not part of us. We suffer when we identify pain as belonging to us. We are not our sufferings. We are presented direction to transcend our despair through a welcoming adaptation of all that is presented to us. In acceptance of what is, we open our eyes to what we truly have.

When an individual immerses themselves into the safety of the collective identity of society, they become vulnerable to being manipulated by it. The atrocities of our past massacres paint this image and calls into question whether one can claim to be "good" while allowing such events to unfold. As a learned individual who is skilled in the art of rhetoric paints their picture on the world, the creation resembles its origin. The darkness in which we cast within our souls will manifest itself in our character and environment. The only way to overcome such things is through individual action, welcoming all persecution, subjugation, and oppression that it incurs. Let us breed Hitler out of our genes.

Our distorted and abused understanding of the term "belief" has caused much suffering over the course of our human history. A simple modification of the term to not identify oneself within, but instead demonstrate a degree of inclination towards, without limiting the scope of, could solve many of our irrelevant disputes. But can a horse be a man? Our identification of the self is not in this or that but instead a disconnectedness towards the one.

The entire philosophical and religious scope of our human history has been in a process of coming to its realisation. Significant developments can be seen and our human consciousness evolves as a result. Hostility from diversity is seen in our actions which occurs from misunderstandings, misrepresentations, and misinterpretations of the wisdom being conveyed. Regardless of any beliefs or lack there of, every unique individual human being is asked one question at every moment of their existence: What will you do with the given? The answer to this question will determine if one is or is not able to save their soul.

ACT 12
BARBED WIRE FENCES
April 24, 2012

Why do we create fences where there once was none? We are a species that sees the limits of our world and then dedicate ourselves to overcome them. Yet the systems that we erect within society dominate our lives. What can we do to tear down the limits of our experience? How are we able to alter our systems to treat the one in front of them with care and particularity?

The Retard. In the process of stepping back and observing society and its actions, one alienates themselves from it. Repeating this over a nomadic lifetime forms a being that does not resemble, concern, or identify itself with the same or similar matters with any of the collective community. To truly think for oneself is to unknowingly or knowingly choose a life of loneliness, subjugation, and oppression. To find like minds not only becomes a struggle but an impossibility. When one's priorities do not conform to the collective consciousness, they become exiled from their human brothers and sisters. No longer limited by society, faith may act as a tool for the subject so that they can harness their superhuman god-like abilities.

As a result, the creation of themselves and everything they touch will shine brightly. But all the while this faith is in vain, for they will never find what they seek. The treasures of their creations will be overlooked in most cases. If they are not overlooked, society will systematise them placing the content in boxes and distributing them as dogmas. Society then "grows" as a result of these systems which originally came from pure intentions. The human inability to take content without categorising and identifying within it is nothing more than a corruption. Systems dominate our minds, and when no visible and organised systems exist, we make them. Thus we can observe the newly formed graph that can relate to us exactly how we feel or ought to feel, disconnecting ourselves from any actual feeling. The organisation of our minds manifests itself outside of our minds and is then forced upon other people in our world. We spoon feed information that is poisoned from a corrupted perspective. If we do not conform to those expected normalities then we are pushed out of social relationships.

We claim with pride that we live in a "free" society. Unfortunately nothing could be further from the truth. The weapon of oppression is now rarely a sword because the weapon of the consequences of nonconformity has been found to be much sharper and cut much deeper. When the understandings and mental distribution of the collective is directed through media, corporations, and government, we lose ourselves to our surroundings. We model our humanity on the factories that we have created. The noble ideal to give every individual the freedom to pursue their own happiness has been taken away. We now live in a world entirely full of unhappy people and our systems attempt to make this model sustainable. We now think we find happiness through material goods and entertainment, but at the end of each day we sigh as the hole in our hearts remains unfulfilled. We now claim happiness but have lost its understanding, that is the conditions required to necessitate happiness. And our oppressors very well know and even play on this fact.

Adam's Song. Let us look at the human and how it functions. Adam is a biological creature. When he is wounded then he must tend to his wounds in order to recover his health. He lives in a garden and eats the fruits of its environment. He explores the garden to learn its nature. When something is needed, he will employ tools and structures to accomplish his intentions. When he feels hungry he tracks food and dines and when he feels cold he covers up with resources found within his environment. When himself or his environment do not act in accord with his overall well-being, he employs the necessary methods in attempts to transcend the situation at hand.

Now let us examine the problem when we introduce many Adams. Now Adam is among a society of himself and he must learn how to cope with this fact. These other Adams then must fight for their survival because of the limited resources and man power. As a result a nomadic tribal system is formed assigning duties to each Adam. But how are we to keep the peace in such a society? Develop a strong sense of solidarity. Together the tribe may stand strong and because of its relatively small formation, they are able to create a close knit community.

But there exist other tribes who are nothing more than "savages". They must protect their newly formed society with force. They therefore then study their opponents strange lifestyles in order to discredit them, enforcing an 'us and them' mentality. As time goes on the tribal wars continue and the ability to effectively communicate with each other remains an impossibility since they have been enframed to perceive only their tribal members as "real" humans. Truth was the words of the elders and superstition was the paintings in their heart.

Generation after generation continues like this but over time the tribe builds a more accurate representation of knowledge and as a result learn how to cultivate the land. The once hunter/gatherer tribe situates itself on appropriate soil. As a result of this alteration of lifestyle, many new considerations manifest themselves. A conception of property is formed. How are they to protect their land and as a result themselves? And now that they are situated enough to store equipment and food, how are they to distribute it? A conception of ownership of things outside of what is on one's person is formed. And who is the one to administer over such matters? Well that depends on the society's needs at the time and each individual's abilities, most likely a renown warrior.

Remaining within the borders of one area, a town is formed. Each Adam by now has found their role to perform within the new system and this results in class divisions. No more is each a part of the whole because the parts are able to work independently of each other. As a result we have a social disintegration within the community. The farmers do not mingle with the warriors and vice-versa. Each is then assessed on the function they serve and those with power are the measures of the importance of each function.

In time the sustainability of such a system is questioned and the leaders are forced to adapt their approaches in order to obtain and maintain control. As they look around they consider much larger societies. If they are to survive they must break away from their own independence. The rulers of Adam Town depart on their journey to a favoured empire. They shake hands and as they depart they leave with new aristocratic titles. They have traded their beloved community for their new lucrative positions. They now stand as kings who report to the empire in their newly modified society. The land is now owned by the empire that protects them and thus requires compensation. What is owned by one is now own by the empire. Exploitation becomes common practice as a result of either need or greed of the rulers.

Over time technology is developed and as a result so is the market system. Our empire is now able to build factories and manufacture a wide range of products for consumption by exploiting the planet's resources. The printing press encourages an intellectual boom in which new conceptions of everything arose. As the private markets produce and political battles continue, the economy takes shape and a framework is portrayed directed towards capitalism.

Land then becomes a commodity and our humanity is lost in systems. The past systems that have grounded our present one haunt our ability to create effective and caring social structures. In the battle for power our species has divided itself into many different accounts of what a human should be and we therefore become bitter towards certain "types" of people. The constant search for what is in our brother's pocket divides even the closest of us and we isolate ourselves from each other. We form an understanding of the world based from how we are treated and comport ourselves into that role. Our only priorities become the priorities of the collective will. The only choices are to try and get your hand in the pot or become an outcast.

Daily activities become easier when close together so what could be a better idea than to form large cities? The activity becomes too cumbersome for our minds to understand so we retreat into the foetal position and reject understanding of anything. The collective understanding will work best for us, so what motivation do we have to go beyond it? The desire to know about the person in front of us diminishes and our collective will becomes no more than feeding our greedy mouths, obtaining the "ideal" lifestyle through enslavement within employment, and stabbing each other in the back to get there, only truly never getting anywhere.

Damn Fences. We have entirely fenced off our lives. We erect fences around our bodies, minds, and souls. We situate ourselves inside the borders of those fences to gain a sense of security to cope with our situatedness. We desire security as our media has frightened us from going outside. Adventures have been written off as we live out "safe" and "secure" lives. We rarely take chances because of the fences around us, for it is difficult to tell if there is electricity flowing through them.

Let us first remove humans from the equation of our environment. Where can we see fences? We can understand difficult terrain to act as fences and these can possibly be utilised or modified by the presence of life. The oceans act as fences that separate the masses of land and their altitude. Gravity and the atmosphere of Earth also act as fences. We can think of these subjects and understand nature and how it functions. We can also recognise that it is our human nature to jump these fences. We can utilise areas with difficult terrain for particular projects or even alter the terrain. We sail across the ocean with ships. We build space crafts to pierce through the walls of the limits of our own atmosphere. We create air planes to travel the skies. Our list could continue for the limits of our human drive is what we make it.

If we are such driven creatures to go beyond these fences, then why do we create so many of our own? I am a planet walker and have spent countless amounts of time walking through a diverse range of conditions and the one thing that I notice absolutely everywhere is... the fences! These things are seriously irritating! I can walk roads for days or even weeks and get stuck in a jungle of fences. "Private" property has taken over our planet and it is now a hardship for one to just be able to exist and travel by foot. Massive amounts of beautiful wilderness remains cut off from our human experience. And all that is in the way is a fence and a strip of unoccupied private property. And what are we to do? It is extremely rare for me to see a fence that would not be extremely easy for me to pass. However, I do not like performing acts against the law. I see wonderful beauty behind your land and I only desire to get there. But your property says, "NO!" and gives me no opportunity to question with, "WHY?".

I do not desire to perform any acts of hate and only want freedom. Your systems cut that freedom off from me. Let us step back and consider why a fence is closed. Why do you not want me to come to your door? I spent a week before knocking door to door working for a charity and it was terrible. People were so rude and the entire experience was nothing but sad. When someone comes to your door why do you immediately become defensive? Why do we not want others to interact with us? If I am thirsty and come to your door for water, you would probably give with extreme hesitance and suspicion. If I asked for food you would tell me to get a job. And if I was just wandering you would close your door, advising me to keep at it. But I want to be at your door because I have no other doors to go to, and maybe your door could open up a chain of doors for both of us.

But your doors, hearts, and minds, are closed and locked. And you secure them all off with your fences. I stand outside of your fences and stare at the beautiful wilderness behind your property and cry.

Damn Systems. In order to maintain the status quotient, we pigeon hole people with paperwork. We ask leading questions that require a particular lifestyle to be correctly answered. If one stands outside of those questions, a lie must be employed or the product and/or service is rejected. Questions like address, occupation, and phone number are questions that require particular lifestyles in order to be answered. Identification requirements are no different. One is expected to be identifiable at all times and if they choose not to ascribe to this practice then it will cause great controversy with authority figures as well as the rest of our systems.

The rigid structures in your systems have caused me most, if not all, of my hardships within life. You expect a certain type of individual to stand in front of you, and when you stare at one who has deviated, you are unsure how to proceed. In the end you either work around the system's follies by lying to it or sending me on my way.

Conformity is the solution for those with a broken or suppressed spirit. How are we to avoid the systems fucking us over? Become the archetypal image of a person that it expects. Lubricate the cog by accepting the oppression. That is, to alter the self to adhere to the system's requirements. You lose your very self because you do not understand what the systems are doing to you. As a coping mechanism, you create social axioms like, "You can't fight the system" and "There is nothing you can do about it". These understandings then enslave you to continue in your own meaningless existence. You have become the product that society has intended. Great work dear comrade!

I am by far not attempting to rebuke the employment of systems. Quite the contrary. Systems avail seemingly unlimited potential for our species. I am merely shining light on our current systems. When one identifies within these systems, horrible acts can occur outside of them. When these systems rule over us instead of us over them, we enforce conditions on the masses that results in unhealthy behaviour. Our systems then point the finger back onto ourselves for the reasons for this unhealthy behaviour, but nothing could be further from the truth. But it is ingenious to place blame on the individual without considering the background conditions that caused their experience and consciousness to develop as it has. This mechanism will keep us in line and hating each other. What better way to control the masses than to shirk the responsibilities of the systems by placing them on its undesirables. We then form social stigmas and hold them against "types" of people because of course, they are the problem within society. Oh wait, it is actually you that is the problem within society because it is you who carry out and encourage these destructive practices.

Our Nature. What is our nature? What does it mean to live in accord with one's nature? In order to go about answering this question we must stand back and examine what it is that we are and how we function on an organic level. We must remove our cultural understandings and examine the foundations of the human being. We must examine our natural desires and comportment within our environment. Independent of this or that era, we must look at what is and ignore what is not.

We are social creatures that are directed towards love. We live in communities and play a role. We integrate within structures to avoid demise. We are creators and can use our gifts to secure future comforts. We create close social engagements and form relationships. If attraction is reciprocated, we create mutually beneficial unions giving us the opportunity to extend our bloodline. We desire comfort and security and these are brought about by obtaining the most beneficial connections with people who most appropriately fit within our own particular psychology. We strive for what is beyond our capabilities and as a result tend to over time achieve any dream that we so desire. The possibility for our species is to go beyond itself.

We are curious creatures and look into the stars and wonder what they would be like. We closely examine the moon and spend many years developing the necessary conditions needed to be able to travel there and eventually exploit her. The barbed fences only act as a temporary setback to our heart's desires. We examine our surroundings and obtain multiple understandings of the resources of our planet. We then utilise those resources to create and employ tools to assist us in accomplishing our goals. We learn to manipulate these tools in order to further expand the possibilities of the resources that we have been blessed with.

Now let us take this model and apply it to our psychology. We implement systems that have no actual existence within our world, that is they exist only within our own minds. These systems are then employed, maintained, administered, and developed by people. Over time these systems grow and become too large to make significant changes to. There are too many people keeping up with and utilising these systems on a day to day basis to alter its infrastructure in order to reflect the current period of time. The result is disastrous and the system obtains a mind of its own. No longer is the system controlled by anyone but instead it controls the population. The right and left hand are in vertigo.

Developers are reduced to nothing more than patch workers. The systems they work with on a daily basis are too vast to make any true developments to because they do not understand the systems that they work on. It has taken a life form of its own. The amount of redundant functions continuously increase year after year as people leave. The entire system ends up being ran by people who have no idea what they are working with. They are trained to make alterations and add-ons, that is to work on a part. To remove any parts of the system is a vast and unprofitable procedure and is thus usually avoided. But the system itself has gone beyond their control and each day develops another extension that will one day become a functional redundant part, forever growing the enormous monster of our systems that reigns domination of our society. This is our dragon that wreaks havoc on our way of life by scorching it with fire.

If we do scratch an old system and replace it with the new, the migration process still leaves us unsure if things are in order. The new systems developed reflect that of the old because those systems are known. The core policies and procedures remain untouched. Even though stories of the building were demolished and rebuilt, the foundations of our systems remain the same. We piggyback our understandings whether or not those understandings were found to be beneficial. And why? Because to start from scratch, that is from the ideal, is not a profitable endeavour and can take much time if done carefully. But none of that matters. We are only human beings. The all mighty dollar is worth so much more than us. A creation of man becomes worshipped by man and acknowledged to be greater than man. Again I congratulate all the progress we as a species have made. I clap my hands for your handy work. Thank you for doing your part to actualise the current state of our human race.

Representation. Throughout our known human history we have been creators. From the origins of our very nature we are built to create new life. From there we are built to create and employ the necessary tools to minimise discomforts. But we have missed the meanings found within our creations. When we examine our creations we are able to better understand its creator, that is our creations are representations of us. We can build an understanding about our lifestyles through the examination of the fruits of our labours. Our physical, mental, and spiritual capabilities and understandings shine brightly through the essence and functions of our creations. Each artefact tells an extremely long story.

But why has our toils backfired on us? Why do our creations no longer represent divine manifestations? Where did we deviate from true health of humanity? This question can be answered when we consider that all creations are manifestations of their origin. And what has our origin become? The problematic manifestations of our society comes from the systems of our past piecemealed together. Over time these layers of sediment form themselves as the foundations of our own thinking. The system is the best because it and everything that we have ever known has always functioned in that manner. We are indoctrinated into the understanding that these systems are effective methodologies to employ and satisfy our creative and social desires.

As a result, we create while adhering to the confinements of our systems. Our creations then represent its creator as the creator has no mind of their own. The psychology of one closely relates with the psychology of the other because they have both been enframed in the corruption and confinement of human ability. The result we are left with is an inferior product. A product that has made its way to you as a result of the corrupt and oppressive system that you have ascribed to. The results of your labour does not represent an ideal individual but a brainwashed one. And this representation stands as an accurate portrayal of its creator.

Conclusion. What does it mean to go beyond our own limitations? Why do we create limitations when none exist? If we are beings that can walk on the moon then why can we not walk on the soil of the wilderness behind our private property? How are we to tear down our fences?

The answer to these questions lie in Descartes' Meditations and post-modernism. We need to demolish our structures. We need to rethink our systems carefully and create strategies to resign our old ones. We need to look around our world and make some decisions as to how we should live our lives with all our brothers and sisters within our environment. We should implement systems that are designed to respond immediately to its wounds and then develop the system taking into account the inconsistencies that it found. "The system will not let me" needs to be replaced with red flags and a referral to the developers who can resolve these inconsistencies and thus remedy the problem for all future scenarios. Cases with vast background conditions need to be handled with care and particularity.

Our education systems need to become more holistic. As a result of the industrial revolution, we have each taken on very specific fields of study. This in itself causes our minds to close and our attention to only be focused on a particular area. All the while we lose sight of the bigger picture and this causes mistakes to be made that will disintegrate our community. This is because absolutely everything relates with everything else. If we only study one particular field, the integral relationships that other fields of study have to and from your own field of study is lost. In the end we are left with a faulty component that is plugged into the system only waiting to malfunction when the necessary conditions for its malfunction are met. Each field of study is many fields of study and these relationships will further expand seemingly forever, that is if one chooses to put in the time to become, a superman.

ACT 13
THE MARKS OF HUMANITY
July 12, 2012

How will we respond to a solid attempt to enable the conditions required to employ effective teaching systems within our society? When all that is needed has been laid before our feet, will we kick away the priceless stones or nurture and protect them? How are we able to change the world when we overlook what is right in front of us? Will us humans ever learn how to realise the potential that we right now hold in our hands.

Welcome to Atheden. This is now our new utopian society. It is as fast as the turtle but always wins the race. It is not said to be this or that but instead develops from within and reaches out into all of society. Among its beautiful and never ending gardens you will come to understand its nature which will persuade your feet to align within its circle, because you will come to understand that your nature derives from It. This will result in your passion, desire, and dedication to exist as and within the highest form of It understood and actualised into your existence.

When our errors have been identified and methods to correct those errors have been conveyed, who then holds the responsibility to make a better future? Are we as humans doomed to wallow within our sins or do we have the ability to go beyond them? Are we going to reject what is strange just because it is new? Are we going to continue to live out the lives that our government enforces upon us? Are we going to continue to indoctrinate the masses or instead teach them how to think for themselves? What is our responsibility when everything that we need to achieve our Atheden lay in front of us but only in pieces. Are we able to go beyond our follies by evolving with beneficial change or we always going to be confined by the straight jackets that our governments entangle us into?

This morning I met a girl and the first thing that she said to me was, "I love you". It is only when each individual and as a result the collective freely expose their hearts in this manner that we will ever be able to free education. These are the necessary conditions for this evolution. We can ride this wave out or build corruptions into it. Our next actions will determine the course of our future and potential human history.

When every human being in this world has virtually an unlimited amount of knowledge at their fingertips available in many receptive and convenient formats, we forever change the direction and practices within our cultural make-up. The facilities and intuitively dynamic interfaces provided to students can enable their own minds to expand as far as they have the dedication to take it. Time becomes of little relevance as all the methods can be integrated easily into individual schedules and lifestyles. And those who entirely dedicate themselves to it will have the opportunity to feed any intellectual, emotional, and spiritual desire. This will eventually result in building a society where the character of an individual is judged by their abilities and not their social order. The most important and controversial issues of all time will be placed back on the table and we as a society will be prepared to solve them. The bigger picture will slowly be revealed as we develop stars within these systems who invest into very specialised areas. Our words will once again be contrasted with our actions and we will all find out whether we can practically apply our understandings. We will exist together in our nature and become part of the divine creation.

Each man and woman has now been given the keys to their dream car. Now we must learn how to drive it. If we are careless in our actions then we will ultimately cause our own destruction. We have been given the transport required to reach any destination that we so desire. How much time will we invest into building a perfectly integrated system? How many driving courses must we take before we are confident to travel on the road? Will we throw away human decency and cause chaos upon our new world that encapsulates an infinite amount of potential? Will we ignore the need for traffic regulations to guide us along our way? Or will we build effective and caring structures to direct our individual and collective potential towards healthy forms of mental distribution?

The world we live in is huge. There exist so many different types of people and a lifetime of exploring would not be long enough to comprehend them all. We have now created a virtual world that can help us locate and communicate with those who function most appropriately with our own particular psychology. Technology has tumbled down the walls of our limiting structures and all the necessary conditions are now enabled to reach our potential. We are now able to spend our lives searching for the right people and as a result those who do, will one day reach all of their potential. Our friendships are no longer bound by the distance of our location, but now we are given the ultimate tool for humanity.

Each major technological development is fine tuned and eventually effectively integrated into our society. We first used natural resources to pass down our interpretations. We then invented the printing press that enabled knowledge to be distributed cost effectively. The need for communication during war brought us to our developments in electronic highways of information. And from this corruption we slowly shed the dead skin and transform it into a virtue. We iron out the problems of this new technology and as we do this our interfaces improve efficiency As we learn the new systems, we become accustomed to how it all works. And as a result we learn how to become better people. We develop holistic understandings with its manifold and are then encouraged to interact in a loving mentality to support and lead its development and direction.

We live in the year 2012 and the world is ending. A new world is about to begin if we only allow it to unfold. We have learned the theory on how to create a utopian society. We now only need to figure out how to put it all into practice. We might start with education to achieve our enlightened perspectives but the means and the ends are two different equations. To lead our future to our desired outcome we must figure out a path that will get us there. And on this road we will travel many directions, but in the end we will prevail or fade away out of existence. And the road to love is not an easy journey. Love will always conquer all but we will choose whether it will include humanity.

What road rules will you create and follow to ensure safe travel for all on this highway? When we are shown the theory of how we could change absolutely everything then what do our responsibilities become? What about when this theory is put into action and exposed as the gold that it could one day be? We now have a new born child who could change our entire society. How will we treat this child? Will we deprive it of nutrition? Will we deprive it of love? Will we ignore its existence? How will we treat our fellow humans when the truth has been revealed? Now let us spread the good news in order to raise awareness about free education and as a result let us watch the beginnings of our new utopian society. Let us all learn to read between the lines so that we can all write our own stories.

To fix the world we must first fix our minds. To fix our minds we must first fix our hearts.

ACT 14
LOOK IN YOUR MIRROR
April 10, 2012

The systems of our society have a bad habit blaming the individuals within it for problems that it directly caused. Our current mental health practices fail to observe outside of the individual's mind to find reasons as to why people are the way that they are. The collective oppression of society requires certain types of people, and when individuals can not or will not conform, they are cast to the side as insignificant and as a result treated less than human. Isolated and alienated from and by society, suicide becomes the best solution to escape their loneliness.

My time in this world has come to an end. My entire life has been dedicated to physical, mental, and spiritual growth. I have studied love inside and out because I was not blessed with this within family, friends, or any other collective groups. At a very young age I was separated from my parents who did not care. Searching for "love" I found a high school sweetheart who I eventually married. But as time passed, it became obvious that she did not wish to be with a philosopher, so she left me and as a result I also lost all my friends, which were only mine through her. Our love was not healthy, and after she left me, she told everyone that the only reason she was even with me was because when we met I looked like "Hanson", which was her childhood obsession. This left me entirely alienated in a huge world without a soul to lean on.

This disorientation led me to rely entirely on the only thing I had left: God. I gave it all to wisdom, and searched for it everywhere. I travelled around the world and back looking for people who would love and accept me for who I am. I jumped from state to state, city to city, town to town, and university to university searching for people who not only studied wisdom, but demonstrated said wisdom in their actions. But the search was more cumbersome than I expected, for all of you are stuck in your systems and do not leave any room to let the unknown in. You all immerse yourself in collective groups and push out what is not understood immediately, nor do you desire to understand. Your eyes are focused forward and you ignore your peripheral vision. And I am in your peripheral vision.

So I shout out again and again attempting to be noticed so that I might find my place in society. But society mutes my voice by its Aristotelian categories. A system of thought that was created to be utilised as a tool has been corrupted and identified within. You are indoctrinated into the understanding of categories as the only system of thought. Anything that does not fit into your categories you disregard as unimportant. I do not fit into your categories and as a result am your victim. An intelligent and talented individual is cast into the fire because you lack the ability to stand back and consider what is in front of you. And as a result you also cast any possible manifestations of love and particularity into said fire. You burn the Mona Lisa because you do not understand what it is that you are burning. You are the ones alienating me.

You persecute me because I have a message and attempt to preach it. But you have no ears to hear and judge before understanding. Your indoctrination into capitalistic self-righteousness encourages you to be offended if anyone questions your own understandings. Thus your response is to persecute so that you may justify your own lifestyle without critiquing it. We have not learned from our past mistakes as this is only a shadow of the story of Socrates. This is my Crito and you have fed me the new formula of hemlock. Is the opinion of one man who has spent his entire life becoming more than he was less valuable than the collective that places popular culture as their highest good? Our kind merely follows in line with the one in front waiting for our turn to throw ourselves off the cliff. We are nothing more than lemmings unsure who started the trend that will result in the destruction of our species.

I have been writing since I was 6 and when I first started publishing articles no one in my life would read them. You said, "I don't want to read that entire thing!" So I took note and trained my voice and started publishing audio versions of my articles. You then said, "Audio talks are not interesting." I then took note and learned Photoshop and began to publish artwork. You then said, "I don't get it!" I shook my head and contemplated. A little while later many things began to make sense to me and I gained the ability to structure and produce quality educational courses that included fun dramatisations of the topics. Now you say nothing. Now none of you say anything to me. You have run out of excuses and find solace in your meaningless entertainment. Just because you do not listen, does not mean what I have to say is not important. From time to time I get people contacting me (sometimes highly educated) thanking me for sharing my insight. But they are not within arms reach and I remain alone. You just lack the ability to click the button and instead prefer to judge without finding out the details of what it is that you judge. You would much rather watch something that will fry your brain than think. You disregard the expression of one who is right in front of you and find consolation in immersing yourself in material from someone you will never know.

I have grown into a silver tongued warrior. I can talk my way in or out of any situation. Authority figures such as the police and security officers fear my voice. And all I do is shed light into our own stupidity by reiterating what it is that we are doing while speaking with authority. I have studied logic and can create arguments with solid foundations. I run circles around people physically, mentally, and spiritually. The results of dedicating my entire life towards self-development has manifest itself and now most will retreat or persecute and then retreat. I was once stomped all over by you people for my passion but inability to effectively express myself. But now you run. And all I have ever been doing is trying to share a message that will help humanity, that is help you. I love all of humanity but I do not at all love its current state. We are beings that are capable of reaching god-like characteristics, but instead of aiming for this noble pursuit, we immerse ourselves in the mundane of society. From your constant persecution over my lifetime, I have learned how to stand up for myself with logical arguments to back up my premises. I have attempted to utilise this to point people to my website so they might learn why they are the way they are and have fun doing it. But when your own lifestyle might be in question by another who knows what they are talking about, you run before your eyes can have a peek. Sleepwalking with your eyes closed on the highway of life will have its ramifications, and each step you take is only buying you time. If our species does not open its eyes it will be ran over by evolution.

To think for oneself also entails feeling for oneself. Your systems disconnect you from these feelings. You learn whatever the government approves you to learn through the system that they desire to implement. This system separates education from love. These systems have no room for love, but doesn't this separate us from our humanity? Within love we feel. When we take it away over the course of our entire education, we become conditioned to also separate education from love. This benefits the capitalistic framework because it breeds out passion. The government wishes you to quickly get educated so that you can immerse yourself in the workforce so that you may benefit them. Passion is dangerous to this system as it might lead to practices that go against their infrastructure. So what better way to suppress this than to create a hierarchy where no one is in charge! Keep everyone keeping everyone in line! Who cares if we no longer know up from down! It is profitable! Who cares if it conflicts with our humanity and casts blackness in our souls, it is profitable. Who cares about the ones that will not or are not able to conform and get run over by the systems, it is profitable. The dogmas of utilitarianism stand strong and people like me get put down as I am the least amount of suffering whose death encourages the greatest happiness. Only one problem. All of you people are not happy. You live day to day for the next material possession and cruelty towards others is accepted as "just how people are". You have been conditioned out of your humanity and now welcome your flaws. Unhealthy interactions from all parties is just, "business as usual". Your habits disgust me.

This outline can be applied to all of our systems and religion is no different. We force our dogmas upon everyone we encounter. I support most understandings when taken in their metaphorical context, but people stick to their dogmas. Christians do not accept me because I do not accept the Bible as absolute "Truth" nor do I accept Paul's interpretation of "Jesus as God" and as a result the churches interpretation of the Trinity. Jews are more cultural and have laws that one must conform to everywhere as a result of Moses. Muslims do not accept me because I do not accept the Qur'an as absolute "Truth" or Muhammad as the last prophet. Buddhist do not accept me because I do not unquestioningly accept the Eightfold Path as always being appropriate as I am a man of faith. However, I learn as much as I can about all religions and attempt to see the metaphorical meanings behind them so that I might make the best decisions that I can, giving me many perspectives to consider when an event takes place where their wisdom would increase my options. Organised religion does not accept me as I am, for their systems are constructed to change me. I would have no problems with any of their understandings if they had no problems with my own. But just as within any system, what does not fit is constructed to eradicate. The clock is not considered functional if one of its pieces are temperamental. Our species is not a clock.

Teachers (especially in universities) do not care about you. They only care to get their material out and afterwards cut ties with you. They want as little interaction as possible with you. Their ability to effectively teach is diminished because there is no love in their actions. The board of education ensures this is the case by enforcing strict regulations. How is the system to discourage revolt? By overloading the teachers with students! Keep their time booked so they are unable to think about where they step. What a great idea! The lashes on the teachers back eventually condition the teachers but deep down they hold resentment. And what better way can they express these emotions than by demonstrating their discontent with the board of directors directly onto their students? They can be as heartless as those who are just as heartless to them and they worked hard for that right. And this system is then repeated on the student. The student will then either choose to quickly complete their desired qualification or work themselves up the ladder so that they one day might also be able to become as incessant as their professors.

The authority figure intimidates us, for they have an effect on our own lives. We do not look at these figures like ourselves but instead treat them as beings on a pedestal. We put masks on and keep most topics off the table while in the company of these figureheads. We learn how to live different lives depending on the company that we are in. We throw away the ideal of impartiality and divide the self into many categories, some defined by us and others defined by our systems. If one breaks out of this self-destructive practice then they reap the consequences. The social norms of what is "appropriate" comes out and we are punished. But what if we do not care about punishment? Why do we dislike punishment so much? What is really so bad about it? Have you lost yourself? Nay, just the opposite, you have stuck with yourself. What is it really that our oppressors have taken away from us in punishment? Anything that truly matters about us is retained throughout the entire duration of our punishment. If we accept all punishment incurred then its conception begins to break down. Punishment can be encouraging as it can remind us that we have not sacrificed any parts of ourselves.

But have I not backed myself into a corner here? It would appear that I am preaching both particularity and impartiality, but as with everything, the essence lies in its synthesis. If we practice particularity with the individual (and not their title) standing in front of us, we are thus being impartial. We can always have our cake and eat it too, but our systems which dominate our minds preach the impossibility of this. Our systems limit us and greater truth always lies somewhere in between two polarisations.

Today I had my first appointment with the mental health services. They have been attempting to get their hands on me from various locations over the past year. I am very weary in dealing with them because last year they removed me from the freedom of the beautiful wilderness and incarcerated me for six weeks and forced drugs upon me that made me feel absolutely terrible. They ignored all my words and wrote me off as being crazy. So over the four day weekend I prepared a session to force them to listen and took precautions so they would not be able to repeat this terrible event. I was enduring through it because I recently applied for disability and was thus required to work through the systems. I arose before sunset and walked many hours happily prepared to open their ears to my condition. Within a short period of time it became obvious to me that they too would not listen, for their systems did not allow for someone like me. I thus departed and had much to think and pray about.

I have no loved ones in my life. I live in the wilderness and that is the only good thing about my life even though sometimes I freeze. The wildlife loves and accepts me for who I am. They do not persecute but instead find me extremely interesting and I feel likewise with them. But I am human and am a social creature. I travel from place to place attempting to find people who will love and accept me for who I am, but in every step I fail miserably as your systems do not allow my existence and you all follow your systems. I have done this pretty much my entire life. "My people" are not out there. I no longer desire to live. But I have thought this many times and always failed to perform the act. I wish to cut across my Phronesis tattoo on my left forearm and bleed out in the wilderness. Phronesis basically means "practical wisdom" and a death like this would accurately represent my life. This meaningful death is my fond ideation.

After my failed appointment I pumped myself up to end my life. But then I thought about why I have not done the deed yet. I had to find the root cause holding back so that I could eradicate it in order to obtain liberation from the cruelty of misunderstanding people. So I talked to God, as I do to think out most of my difficult issues. And it came upon me like a light bulb in a bubble above my head. It is the systems. I have spent my life to break free from the chains that society has shackled me to but was still connected in a few aspects. I found the root cause. I was usually able to purchase bread, cigarettes, and occasionally as a treat, soft drugs. The systems within university also kept me going when all along I have desired to independently study. These four things chained me to life. They have kept me going enough to continue my lonely existence. And how do I obtain these things? Through systems. I then spent the next few hours walking to Centrelink who financially support my existence because I study at university. Along the way I cut up all of my identification. When I got there I cancelled everything and when I departed I laid the pieces of my identification on their table and asked them to dispose of it. I walked out proud of myself for doing the deed. I cut the life force off which has previously provided just enough to get me through life. I am now free from everything. University, you no longer concern me. I now have nothing whatsoever to fall back on to continue existence except suicide. This act has given me just enough time to make my final statement to society before I depart this world. This article is a part of the course "My Reflected Death", available at nesmith.net. Let my death force you to listen to my words and make a statement so that our species may evolve.

ACT 15
TIME WEAVING
December 27, 2013

How can I tell you the creation story in a way that you would understand? Everything one touches will ripple into time and space. Those with good fruits its masters and those with bad, slaves. For the energy that escapes each individual will be released into their world as they interact with it. From bad will cause decay and from it a new species.

Another book that wrote itself: exactly like the feature film it is based upon. Merely a vessel to collect, order, interpret, and distribute. A simple reflection of a divine image. The nine cycles of my soul articulated to learn how to control them. A puppet master playing its organic heart strings. A failed attempt at resuscitation but a success raising the dead. Setting myself up to go forward in time to warn myself what was about to happen.

A public domain time machine that can go forward without you having to risk your body. The most meaningful thoughts sent as a message to not only me but all hearts like me. The ultimate message in a bottle game that is guaranteed to result in both your life and your death. And when the right bottle comes back to me, I will then be in a position to act on its philosophy.

The heart of each social dysfunction will be judged. Those who were incorrectly judged guilty before trial will be given another chance. All that society has, does, and can offer will be placed on the table. And those who are rulers because that is what they are, will stand a round its table. And the noble will justly command the peaceful army of Love. Misunderstandings as a result of not wanting to learn will sever one species into two. And the mutation will claim back their origin of Love.

Since all of these terrible violations of my human rights played out, I have been in consistent contact with those who administered them. From the Ballarat stockade into the grips of both our physical and mental model of medicine. I keep requesting my files so that I can publicly release them but I am treated as crazy as their system truly is.

I have no secrets. Difficult topics require the right viewpoint and time to be expressed. I have done nothing wrong nor will do anything wrong. My character and how I demonstrate these topics clearly articulates this.

There is a society that my heart truly wants and there is a society in which I know we can achieve. If it were up to God, Its greatest creations would unite physically, mentally, and spiritually when they are ready. Because of the way society currently views the topic of attraction to youth, our ages in marriage might have to be closer to that of society's standards. But the world that is in my heart throws age into its perspective. And when both parties feel confident in their abilities and desires to sexually satisfy one another, then in that first act I now claim to be marriage and not permissible unless both the spirit and mind are synced into one aspect. It is the freedom to unite two of its own parts into the one that they were destined to become: ordained by God and not man. Although my actions will only stretch the borders, my intentions are to destroy them for future generations.

Who is man to interfere in divine Will? The Will to Power...

A shuriken board called life. And from our known artillery, we will be able to spray a custom crafted attack before the fact that was assembled for this very moment. Year after year, my own fireworks light up the skies with hope because I can deconstruct and then reconstruct any part of the puzzle of life and that ability took my worthless life to obtain. But from it I can now weave stories that play deeply within the heart of every human. And

78

some of you will be entertained. Others frightened. And as the true warriors shed their last tear, the spirit will be released and its pain begins a process of maturity. If you are looking at me then you have been tricked by the book's scythe. A real life example will begin to unravel your own responsibilities. And if the chain linked around your own neck becomes your jewellery, then at least now you are aware of this fact.

ACT 16
MONKS SING
May, 2011

Being culturally enframed from birth into an entirely Western culture, one might easily miss purpose found within an Eastern tradition. These writings will focus on the monk. Our Western minds shudder at the thought of the word, "homeless". Preconceptions about what reality is strain the minds about what is acceptable or even possible. Beliefs become scattered or hostile as one attempts to think of another who does not support the economy. This is not to say that a monk cannot support the economy or have a home, and in today's society it becomes difficult to exist without conforming to some degree.

Monks do indeed serve a purpose, and a very vital one for that matter. These writings will paint a picture of what a modern day Western monk might look like. It is not defining any particular man or woman and only stands as an indicator. To know the monk, we must query the monk.

Monks amongst Western society do exist and it is the purpose of these writings to show how, why, and for what means. To dedicate one's life to such a great life force is an extremely rewarding involvement. Just because we are stamped as a "Westerner" does not mean this life path is unavailable to us.

Written shortly before the Ballarat abduction:

Psalms 23

The LORD Is My Shepherd
A Psalm of David.

1   The LORD is my shepherd; I shall not want.
2   He maketh me to lie down in green pastures:
he leadeth me beside the still waters.
3   He restoreth my soul:
he leadeth me in the paths of righteousness for his name's
sake.
4   Yea, though I walk through the valley of the shadow of
death,
I will fear no evil: for thou art with me;
thy rod and thy staff they comfort me.
5   Thou preparest a table before me in the presence of mine
enemies:
thou anointest my head with oil;
my cup runneth over.
6   Surely goodness and mercy shall follow me all the days of
my life:
and I will dwell in the house of the LORD for ever.

Diet. A monk lives in the life force. As a result, the ethical question being what the monk should eat is raised. A monk is a free thinking individual who has investigated themselves, learning and understanding different sides of the arguments and its particulars. Only then one is best equipped to make a decision as to what one shall eat. This is an extremely important subject since we are speaking of removing the life of another sentient being. The subject of a perceived awareness is brought into question: Is it okay to go against the interest of other beings that have also been brought into existence in a similar way that we have while given a similar objective: to stay alive. To remove a life where life once was is a noteworthy decision that needs a great amount of research, prayer, thought, and reflection every time one decides to take a life. To remove from the pool of the life force is to stamp out parts of one's true self.

It is this responsibility and burden that has been given to man every day of their lives since animal meat is not an essential dietary need. The monk will know what it is that they are doing, eating or not. Any food that a monk consumes is blessed, if not by direct prayer, by the conscious knowledge of what it is that they are doing and why it is that they are doing it. They travel in the Lord, and goodness and mercy will follow them all of the days of their lives. Their light inside will shine and they will accept all trials and tribulations because they know they are extremely purposeful. At times greater insight may be given to a particular individual to assist the unveiling of the universe - for all to become, however, a monk does not want nor cling to manifestations from the physical finite world. What comes into existence will also part from it.

Growth. A monk is like a tree in the forest. Many more exist around it, but it does not use those other trees as stencils to what it should become. It becomes what it is. When one is shown a picture of a forest, all trees could be said to look the same - this is until we place ourselves in front of the tree and assess what it is that we are truly looking at. We are then given a much greater perspective to see how truly unique that tree is.

If we are to assert that one is only a product of their physical experience combined with their mental interpretations and reactions to those experiences, we are left with a shell. A machine that has been programmed to respond to conditional states. We become reduced to unthinking reaction based life-forms.

The picture that gets painted and slowly but surely makes itself known. We are able to piece together the puzzle of life intellectually, but this misses something integral. As if we are able to piece together thick borders of the puzzle in question, but a large circle in the middle remains. To expand those borders leaving its middle exposed is of little value. To solve this problem we must shine the light on the conditions of the problem. Where are the puzzle pieces to fill the whole? To find them one must jump directly into said hole.

In life and throughout all things we must grow. Good trees will produce good fruit. We are led back to the "Ideal Man".

Religion. Nietzsche claims that God is dead. What is missed by our current society is what insight his assertion had to offer. Our cultural and religious preconceptions stand in front of us holding a red flag. One is confronted by the way that they understand life. One tends to flow through their life until a red flag is waved at them, and then the defences of the ego at hand kick in.

For one to place their own judgements about the world aside while hearing out another's is a rare character trait to possess in the Western world of today. But why? Jesus' dying words on the cross explained that it was ignorance that held him to the cross. One of the main goals in Buddhism is to remove all ignorance from the soul.

How is it that one can claim to be following their religion when they quickly judge and condemn that of another? How can one preach peace and love and practice its contrary? It is like pointing ahead while walking backwards, teaching all others to do the same. Talking the talk and walking the walk seems to be few and far between in a world where the Church is just as accepting as an exclusive club.

Noticing one's reactions has been driven to a science. As lips vibrate the observer can be seen to go through many different stages. Lips start and finish all wars. All have been trained to make judgements every conscious second because they understand that what they do in the second will effect what has happened before and what they will do next, resulting in the conscious second that they actually live. As Kierkegaard says, "Life can only be understood backwards, but must be lived forward". Or maybe all have been trained to not truly understand this, but compartmentalise them into understood realities. For example, most I speak to understand their past to be the most true reality, but when I further probe their understanding of their past, I receive clear misunderstanding of its conceptual purpose: to orientate. Many identify with their past as if it is material and tangible, when in fact it is nowhere to be found and certainly no more real in the present as Santa Clause or the Easter Bunny. Many obsess over this "past" and focus on it like it was the now.

To live in the past is to bring about failure. To bask in what once was is to miss what is in front of you. To identify with a past you, possession, or/and environment is directly placing limits on you as the individual. One is induced to, as Kant says, a "self-incurred tutelage". We are hypnotised by a sequence in which the function has been overlooked. We escape the concept of the now by identifying ourselves by our past. One watches a television show or a movie not living in the conscious second, but obsessing about the past seconds that added up to the complete picture that the piece of entertainment wished to communicate.

Drug addictions can also work in this manner, where one is always pushing to feel better than they did before, entirely missing what they are presented with in the now. Any time that we identify with the past results in us, missing what we have been presented with right now, and now, and now...

We often find those who obsess over the past to be extremely thorough in their actions. Each conscious action is geared towards topping some past conceived result, thus rituals become important to this individual. The rituals intent is to have better and more than in the past, and every conscious action somehow reflects this.

We also find those who hypnotise themselves with the seducing sound of the future. Those who obsess over what will become. Many of these individuals could be highly motivated and appear as extremely successful in life, but in fact are induced by their own self-incurred tutelage. To create the most in the future while suffering today so that one can avoid suffering in the future, but unfortunately that future never comes. It remains an ideal that forever changes because the ego always searches for more. To be content with one's place is not the ego's function. This results in the grass always being greener on the other side.

When one objective is achieved, that objective is forgotten and taken for granted while another objective has been put in place. It is like we are walking with a hat that mounts a stick with a carrot on the end. We always reach out trying to grab, but are just out of reach. So we keep walking, desiring to get closer to the carrot instead of sitting down and taking the hat off.

Within today's Western enframing, we are discouraged to ask difficult questions. When a child comes to his parent and asks, "Why?", we shy away from them and mark the topic off as infinite regress. To fill the gap we have formed religions that act as a system of beliefs that one can trust, to whatever extent one needs to overcome their fear of that froth on the beer - the wash of the ocean.

And this religious enframing gets stamped into our heads, to whatever extent. And one's current beliefs about what they think is real and imaginary are at least a good portion inherited. One might be seen to finding "different" gods and even fighting, "Holy Wars" over who believes in the same manner. Where God was once love, cultural understandings corrupted and made God a bloody weapon. As long as diversity was like a football game, all stands happy in the Church. When we misinterpret the meaning of the word we have been given, we assert, "I am right and you are wrong". We have identified our very souls within a certain doctrine who adhere in a particular way, that have been translated by one of many ways. As if in a busy train station picking which train will get them home, but only having one ticket to use your entire life. Possibly a little pin the tail on the donkey being played.

We must turn our attention to the conceptual purpose for religion: to fill the gap that nothing human can explain. One is required to, as Kierkegaard would say, take that leap of faith into all that which is unexplainable, for both the conceptual and phenomenological misapprehensions that we possess. Like if we were to stand on a cliff, we would not only be fearful of falling off, but also if we were to throw ourselves off, because we could indeed choose to do that. That force stopping us from jumping becomes the haze of that which could or might be, but that which is not. Every second that we spend on the tip of that cliff, we choose to not jump.

Faith is asserted as spiritually taking that leap, accepting all the paradoxes which it involves. If we spiritually take this leap of faith we become something outstanding. A being that once existed in its froth is now transmuted to a more perceptually aware entity. And as we spiritually grow, we can learn to ride through life in the spirit while utilising our bodies and minds as Godly tools: not to identify directly with them.

Unfortunately "The Word" gets translated from the words by which have been written by spiritually inspired individuals, who lived in a particular culture with a particular series of events that have allowed for that person to be the given certain insight to perform the writings which then get interpreted, misinterpreted, corrupted, forced upon, and made into what it is all together not. The syntax and/or semantics are identified with and argued over, while the true message gets overlooked. Because of our enframing, we are taught to bobble our heads when anything is presented to us, unless it opposes what we have ourselves been taught to value. Our perceptions and values change as we move through life, and as they do, if we are observant, we can realise that investing too heavily in the finite (what is one day may not be another) is worth infinitely more when invested into the infinite.

One might now bring into question what this "spirit" thing is and how does it work? What substances can we truly rely on in this world? Descartes gave us the pictures of two worlds, an internal one (res cogitans) and an external one (res extensa). We then dive into what is known as a theory of knowledge. What can we truly know? What are the implications of what I truly know in comparison to what another truly knows? Subjectivity becomes an enemy to those who refuse to be contented with that leap of faith, to accept what is for what they understand it to be. Science kicks in and gives us great benefits, but still cannot break the subjective barrier because everything that is ever perceived is perceived by a subjective being. Science can never bake its cake and eat it too because its primary intent: to skip the subject.

Each are unique individuals who were born from two forms of DNA, raised in particular environments and are suggested a certain way to live life depending on our external influence. Aquinas asserted that our rituals will be a direct product of our past experiences and influences. This is our enframing which we are held captive. This is the misapprehension: a direct misinterpretation of the real world resulting in quick judgements about a topic one might know little about. The ego kicks in, wanting to be more than it is. Upon understanding, we are enlightened and no longer held captive by its powerful grip. The light bulb brightens our room and the ego is shown to be a sheet draped over a chair.

A magic spark occurs and two become three (or more). The addition is then nourished and kept healthy almost involuntarily. A baby is born and forced upon its carer. From that moment on, the physical aspects of the child begins to develop. For healthy terms, the carer is expected to love and cherish that child as it grows to form a healthy adult. They develop highly tuned skills in the things that they do most often. After some time the child develops intellect and allows the physical self to go on auto pilot while exploring their mental self. They will then explore their mental self through their physical self. The child orientates itself within the world, affirming through repetition the realities of it. Feet go on the ground, hat goes on the head, sky is up, can't breathe under water, what music to listen to, what doctor to go to, what to worship, how to love, how to hate, how to fit in, what to do to fit in. And ones place is generally handed to them by where they get the most encouragement, usually being because of their exceptional abilities in said duties. We become a result of physical and mental conditioning, produced by our environment and the choices that we make.

We see the results of the mysterious subject of love. We at least at some point in our lives remember being loved: paternal, friendships, partners, lovers, animals, nature, and humanity. The cliches about life being a journey or life being a road that one must walk ring true in and out because of our balance that we choose to utilise between our physical and mental, and how much we have identified ourselves with each one. But what gets overlooked in this entire picture is the entity behind the wheel of this dualistic enframing we are given and practiced as a matter of habit. We are now in a clearer (or messier) fog that can point to the presence that the spirit consists of and we are directly presented the question: Why? The last words of Jesus prayed, "forgive them father for they know not what they do", one must ask themselves, "Why do I do what I do?" To remove fear we must learn, to resume control one must live. To truly live is to be awakened as to what it is we are talking about, to know why it is we do the things we do. We have broken from our shackles when we live in the spirit: knowing that those shackles were only created by the mind and if one learns how to use their physical and mental as mere tools, without attaching itself too tightly to any which one but only using them to broaden understandings of what it is that we are truly doing throughout our day to day lives.

Just as Jesus died for the insanity that each human is capable of, putting a man to death when he did only right. His blood was shed to gift us with the ability to transcend suffering. An ability to ride the wave of consciousness and that is through the spirit: the headquarters to line up the planets and become what you truly are. To become the being that is your spirit trying to shine out from you every single second.

As far as investment into something more than the finite comes to great value when preconceptions and taboos are lifted. We realise that one can only ever see what is directly in front of them; a limited confinement of what it is and what everything else is. As Descartes suggest, our senses do in fact deceive us, again and again. So what can we truly rely on? One just might need to take that spiritual leap of faith to find out - to experience and know what it is that you are dealing with. When dis-identification occurs, and one turns around to paddle down stream, one is able to recognise the spirit behind what is being said and by whom. The interactions one makes within society become soft and particular. We are not speaking to just a person but something much more. We are dealing with a grand part of the universe that each and every subject of query has an important purpose and will fulfil whether one swims up or downstream.

One can choose to be a servant to its cause and become something grand, or remain dormant and closed. Either way one looks at it, the interaction between two spirits is a much different conversation between two commoners. Their value is treasured for exactly who they are because they do serve a purpose. Whether the other recognises the master crafting that spiritual conversation has, and what joy it brings. We are able to break the chain of identifying people with numbers as soon as we shine the light to the magic that is really involved. To serve God is to serve people, and to serve people is serving God. In serving people we serve that grandness that God has sparked and connected us with. To most efficiently serve the people one must learn how to first become masters of themselves, to rule over their physical and mental so that they achieve understanding to live in this exact manner, consciously evaluating how you feel about my words, how you are going to interpret them, and what, if anything, are you going to do about it? To become thinking individuals who seek out answers for ourselves. To control the path that is walked. One can choose to do nothing, but in doing nothing one is still doing something. To take responsibility for yourself mentally, physically, and spiritually, in each 'now' moment that passes. To embrace subjectivity for its utility while striving for objectivity, that realm of the spirit.

To shine to the world we must have a fuel to burn. Fuel within the physical wears out, disappears, decays, breaks, and dies. Fuel within the mental can act as an ongoing battle believing one thing one day and another the next, based on greater understandings of the subject at hand. To worship this physical is to misunderstand the nature of the physical. To worship the mental is to rely on the intellect to get through the ever changing maze. When one worships the spirit and its ramifications, one's values begin to shift - align with their true nature. When we learn and live in the spirit we not only study to improve our physical and mental understandings, but place ourselves in the position where we can be of most use in every single situation. To not expect anything out of anyone or anything while welcoming all encounters as God's beautiful plan unfolding, places us in a position of responsibility and power. To take off one's rose tinted glasses to see the world for what we truly perceive it to be empowers us to truly be ourselves so that we can shine as the unique and wonderful individuals that we are, and not the mundane that society tells us to be. Through the spirit, all things are possible.

ACT 17
THE PSYCHIATRIC MODEL
May 8, 2013

Throughout our human history we see terrible acts occur as a result of collective oppression. We like to think that we have gone beyond our past mistakes but unfortunately nothing could be further from the truth. The biomedical model of medicine has reigned sovereign in our current society. But we look away from its follies as it only affects those on the margins of society.

Psychiatric Hospital, Canberra, Australian Capital Territory, Australia
Monday, April 30, 2012

All of my assertions have proven their validity. Everything that I have expected to come to pass within this mental institution has rung true. The hand of the collective arrogance and ignorance spits in my face and refuses to listen. They play games in attempts to get my voice to crack, yet they ignore the voice of my pen and website. Their own conditioned understanding as how a person should be closes their eyes to a creature like myself. Their hearts are cold and their judgements cruel.

The last time I was in a place like this, no one would listen to my words. My voice would be cut off right when they believed that they had accumulated enough information. This caused them to twist my words. So this time I am mute. But my voice is my pen and my website. But they ignore both. Their ears are as closed as their hearts.

On Friday I turned myself in. They took me to the emergency psychiatric department. Here they allowed my possession of my pen and paper for communication. Locked within a small communal area, they gave me no room. I was extremely tired and was given no place to lay down my head. After many hours of sleeping on the bare floor in the hallway, they placed me in a room. They advised me to not close the door as I would then be locked in.

I closed the door and they opened it. I kept locking myself in until they gave up. In the night a doctor came and promised me half an hour of his undivided attention. After about five minutes of listening to an article of mine he exposed himself as the liar that he was. He had no room in his systems for me. I shut down and he lost the communication of his patient. He was not interested in my website nor me, but only what he thought that I should be.

After a night locked in my room, the morning came and a psychiatrist brought me into a meeting room. He attempted to force me to speak. He was not interested in communicating via writing. He was not interested in my website. He followed the ridiculous protocol of questioning: "Are you physically well?", "Do you hear voices or see things that are not there?", "Do you do drugs?", etc... After it became obvious that he would not listen, I wrote on some paper, "You are ignorant. nesmith.net" and placed and origami black swan on the paper in his lap and walked out. Shortly after, they forced me into a wheel chair and loaded me up into a white van headed for a more permanent holding facility.

Now was the time for them to bring out their guns. They stripped me of all my belongings including my pen and paper, that is my ability to communicate. Their systems could not cope with alternative methods of communication so they used their collective oppression in attempts to break me into speech. But there is no choice as my decision was final. Instead they provide me with nothing and wait until I came to them with my needs, but I need nothing and they will never hear my voice treating me like this.

Tonight they attempted to get me to take medicine that remained nameless. I refused so they employed five heavy built guys to hold me down and shoot their drug into my backside, even though my body was not resisting. Before the shot they heard my voice for the first time as I prayed, "Forgive them Father, for they know not what they do." As they take their leave, the world goes hazy and I cry.

The days pass and I lose sight of time. I believe it to either be Sunday or Monday. Over time I have acquired back a few of my belongings. Today a group of five people with my allocated psychiatrist took me into a meeting room. I handed over a letter that I had written specifically for them. They passed it around, not reading it but only glancing at it with arrogance in their hearts. After ten seconds I am handed back the two page letter that I handed them. They then told me that I needed to vocally speak or they would leave. I put down my paper and pen and got comfortable in my chair insinuating that I would do no such thing. That was the end of my first appointment that lasted no longer than one minute. Ten minutes later a nurse came out to tell me that I would be here until I talked to them with my voice. I wrote, "Then I will be here forever". She said, "But don't you want to go home?" and I naturally replied, "I have no home".

And now even though they have given me back my pen and paper, they ignore me. Hitler's orders to ignore my written communication entirely isolated me. My requests for basic necessities such as a tooth brush and tooth paste were ignored. My humanity is entirely ignored without my voice backing up my words. My hygiene deteriorates and they would make note of this in my file. But they were the ones who refused to provide me with the equipment to maintain it. Does a voice make a human? Is the vibration of vocal chords true value?

I will not compromise myself and thus will not put down my pen. Today I started a hunger strike. As expected they do not care. To them I am only expressing a temporal mind set. They believe that collective oppression will crack me. They obviously do not know me. May God be with me for the next seven days. Those are always the hardest to get through when fasting. May God fill my stomach with His spirit. May the follies of our systems be exposed for what they are. Let my suffering act as a 'South Park' episode that shines light on our own stupidity. My Lord! Help my sufferings to not be in vain.

Saturday, May 05, 2012

I am on my sixth day of fasting. I am weak and have no motivation to do anything. My spirit has filled my stomach thus far and my appetite has been on my side. I refuse taking the mystery medicine that they force upon me, so night after night I am taken into my room by four or five people. Time and time again they hold down my limp body and inject a buttock with their evil serum that makes me feel horrible.

I have just recently obtained my pen again. The first day of Doctor Moore's regime was to advise all the staff to ignore my writing. This caused all requests for basic necessities to be ignored. I have just recently obtained a tooth brush and tooth paste. The second day my pen was taken away from me. As a result I could not write nor communicate with the staff. The third day my Kindle and MP3 player was taken away from me so that I could not study nor listen to music. Each attempt at subjugation reinforced my understanding that what I am doing is just.

From time to time I do give my voice, but not to the treating team. There are some people who have a heart who are on my side, but the systems place the doctors as the tyrants. But the doctor will not listen to his lackeys. Their drugs not only knock me out but cause discord with my conscious awareness. In addition, these drugs are meant to be taken on a full stomach. But I have found out all too well that these people do not care about my well-being. I am a beautiful person who displays absolutely no psychotic symptoms, but they still drug me. Not a single doctor has communicated with me, yet they still drug me.

They play with people's minds. Time and time again they tell me that they are going to discharge me but this never happens. The lukewarm shower causes me to shiver. Time and time again I request another doctor and/or a second opinion, but each verbal or written request is ignored.

I try my best to keep my sugar levels up but my body desires sustenance. I am unsure if or when I will be able to continue this diary as my body is coping by shutting down. To be a just person I must die on my cross.

Monday, May 07, 2012

This will only be a quick entry. A few more traumatic injections have been and gone. I just finished my hunger strike of seven days. God made me aware that it was time to stop. My tribunal will commence shortly. I have no hopes there though as I am told patients do not win that. I will write more after the tribunal. May God have mercy on my soul.

Monday Night...

Oh my powerful and mighty God! The black swan has been recognised for its colour! The pieces of my life fell together in front of the board and I was powerful. The light was shined on the absurdity of the proposed treatment, which wanted to oppress my body and mind for at least six months. Every reason for the treatment was discussed and debunked right before my eyes.

I not only shined as the divine being that I am, but also touched the souls of the board members. In addition, the boards psychiatrist was versed with the works of my predecessor, Søren Kierkegaard. Today it appears that God might have opened the doors for the rest of my life. They understood everything and I walked out the doors a free man with a clean bill of health who is voluntarily being treated in attempts to carefully be integrated back into society. Every future action will be entirely on my own terms and no longer will I have to worry about drugs being forced upon me. The inhumane shots are a thing of the past and I now possess medical evidence to prove not only my sanity, but also my spirit and intelligence to fight and win against collective oppression. Praise God!

Tuesday, May 08, 2012

I should of never counted my chickens before they hatched. This morning Doctor Moore took me in a meeting room to only arrogantly tell me, "You are being discharged". This was not the treatment that was discussed in the tribunal. We discussed volunteer time in the ward while I am carefully integrated into the community. But since he was my psychiatrist, he could do anything that he wanted. And he was obviously upset about losing the tribunal against me. For the last time I asked for a second opinion which was yet again rejected. I needed to stay until social constructs on the outside world were put in place! I turned myself in for a reason and not only to incur additional trauma to my psychology. I refused to leave and repeatedly requested for them to call the psychiatrist who was on the tribunal board. A few times I caught them in their lies as they said they did call him, but I could see right through them and this was proven when they changed their story to, "we cannot contact him". So they called the massive wards men that usually were the ones holding me down while I was injected to escort me out of the building. I exited but refused to move from the entrance.

They were attempting to relocate me to a boarding house for crisis accommodation. But this is not at all adequate. I am a gentle and loving person but I get ran all over by the sorts of people who reside there. I have been through this procedure before and it has always turned out terribly. There "help" was no help whatsoever but only passing the buck to another to again attempt to force me into the low class of society. Eventually they called security in attempts to force me into the van, but I know all to well the limited rights of security officers and stood my ground. They then called the police. The police then advised me that I could not stay there. Even though it was a public place, since the hospital did not want me there then I was required to leave. So I picked up my bag and started walking. An eight hour walk back to the city and then the university library.

Yet another traumatic experience to attach to my consciousness... And all of this occurred within the most advanced psychiatric facility in Australia, located in Canberra: the country's capital.

Conclusion

Why does our systems not show care or particularity to the people within them? They spit on every human right. They require complete submission to them or drastic consequences will incur. Ethics is thrown out the window and collective oppression is instated as God. Those who deviate from those in power are harshly punished.

How are we to ever develop as a species with these conditions in place? The wrath of our oppressors is mighty. You are likely sitting comfortably within your lifestyle while reading this, but right in front of you situations all over the world similar to this occur. You turn a blind eye to these happenings. You have been indoctrinated into adhering to the tyrant of society but somehow you claim to live in a "free" nation. You develop a sense of pride in your country despite it controlling your every movement. You allow things like this to happen right in front of you. It is likely that you are now thinking that one person can not make a difference, but if you do not stand up to these injustices then no one will.

The reason why things are the way they are is because of you. These systems are your own fault because you lack the courage to stand up and actually make a meaningful life for yourself. You submit yourself to these oppressive and destructive systems and claim that nothing can be done about them. You encourage these systems along by partaking in them through your immersion in the capitalistic framework. You learn to interact in destructive ways by valuing your lifestyle above human flourishing. You blindly accept social axioms without questioning their validity. You take your mystery pill that is handed to you.

Do you want to know how to save your soul? Stand up and fight. Accept your fate whether it be good or bad. Do not sit idly while our world is in such a poor state. Become the best person that you can be by learning the details of our oppressors and striking the systems in the best manner that you know how. Accept your calling by changing the world, one human at a time. And when you become the best you can be you also encourage all those around you to follow suit. Shine like the star you are and accept all punishment that results. This is not a one time deal. This is your life. Make your life make the world.

ACT 18
MY LEGACY
April 26, 2012

Life or death? Irrelevant. The framework in which I was called to employ has been completed. All that is required is for the right set of eyes to examine the fruits of my labour and the possibility of revolutions within many fields of study will manifest. Whether our species has the ability to overcome its problems depends on whether we can exercise care and particularity within our systems. If we remain without care of each other, unable to gain the understanding as to why people do the things they do, then devolution will continue and business as usual within our capitalistic framework will destroy our lives.

I have pioneered the deepest and most dangerous waters of the sea. I have taken the burdens of the world upon my shoulders and made a thorough attempt to resolve them. I have achieved what everyone told me throughout my life was impossible. Every step of the way society has pushed on me the conception that one man can not make a difference. The collective will did not want a pioneer. It did not think possible the grandiose ideals that I have strived for. It laughed at the possibility of the ideal individual that I dreamed of. For I was only a dreamer and their society in which they rest indoctrinated them into believing that dreams could not possibly manifest themselves into our world.

But now you are speechless as I have actualised the

superhuman that I have always dreamed to be. You once mocked my aspirations but now all you can do is stare with your mouths wide open. I am no longer mocked but instead persecuted. The high ideals I have obtained which you claimed impossible are now apart of me and this makes you uncomfortable. When you see for your own eyes the fruits of a truly divine being, you consider your own lives. Upon initial investigation you observe things that make you uncomfortable so you immediately abandon the project. Now standing in front of you is one who has completed that project and you feel inferior.

But since you abandoned the project to examine your own life, how are you to react to me? Your solution is either to stay away from me or persecute me. The need to justify your own life pumps fiercely through your veins and you create irrational methodologies to cope with your own inadequacies. And what better way to justify yourself than to demonstrate yourself to be the exact person that I am explaining to you that you are. The very fact that you feel the drive to justify your own actions with arrogance demonstrates clearly that what I am saying is accurate, at least in your case. Your defence mechanisms are working hard in attempts to sustain the lifestyle that you have chosen. And upon me shining light on your own understandings, your reaction is to protect your current state of existence. Instead of standing back and examining what I am speaking about, you instead burn the flower that stands before you.

Lower your guard my friend and take the punches. For these punches are administered to show you how to be a better human being. When you are a better human being, everybody around you is also a better human being. And there is no pursuit more worthy to our kind than learning how to be better human beings. And I do not tell you how to be this ideal, for that is locked away within yourself. Instead I erect sign posts to assist you to get to where you truly want to be. Drop your fists and open your heart. I am its doctor.

I have scaled to the heights of the roughest terrain of the mountains. I have found God's commandments to be locked within each individual's heart. On top of the mountain God gifted me with a universal key and I now present this key to you so that you are able to make a copy. All that is required of you is to manifest the necessary equipment in order to make a duplicate. You are my comrade and I only want what is best for you. But it is your own conditioned psychology that you must understand before you will notice that this key is made of gold. But you too must obtain the raw material before its mirror image is reachable.

Do you understand? I have completed the basic framework of my calling and now it is up to you. Today I am unable to place force down when I slide the blade over my wrist. Maybe tomorrow will be different but I can only work with the moment. I have gifted you with two courses on the only topics in existence that matter: it and its end. I have outlined and pointed you to not only my perspective, but how you too can achieve your own perspective. I have carried out my God given work to provide you with the means to not only improve yourself, but the world. I have given my all to you so that one day we as a species might become grand. The rest is up to you.

As far as me, I am done with this life. I do not wish to exist. I have learned to no longer care about anything. But God secures my hand away from my wrist and this causes a problem concerning my future. But I guess this too is not really a problem, for I no longer care about it. Every day I will attempt to muster up enough courage to end my life. The past, present, or future is no longer any concern for me. All I must worry about is all this stuff around me as I walk through hell. To live directly and only in the present is my fate. That is if you can call what I am doing, "living".

Tomorrow I am handing myself over to the mental health services who have been attempting to get their hands on me for the last year. I want to make it clear that I am not handing myself over to them for "help". Their systems lack the ability to do that. Instead they can "deal" with me. I understand all too well how their systems function and all that is in store for me there is solitary confinement. But it is you society that has brought about the conditions required to form someone like me. Therefore you will have to deal with me for as long as I live with your own tax dollars. You have given me no opportunities to make a life for myself and as a result I no longer care about life whatsoever. I will play the role that you push on me.

I am through talking. You don't listen anyway. I am cutting my voice in more ways than one. All I have ever done for you people is try and love and help, but your cold hands beat by body lifeless and I no longer trust your intentions nor illogical opinions. It is you that has created this mental patient, for all he ever wanted was your love. So I will give myself over to the very systems that have destroyed my life. I will present my wrists but not my voice. I will no longer concern myself with anything whatsoever. I will be free from your malice and care of your opinions of me. I will live out each moment invested in that particular moment with no concern of anything outside of that. I no longer desire to provide you any content whatsoever because of your constant disrespect. I have completed what it was that I was sent down to do, so now nothing else matters for me. I am more than happy to live out my life entirely mute. It will not be much different than the life that I have lived.

Do you understand what I have done? I have carefully analysed the two polarisations of the human in two university-grade educational courses: life and death. I have covered all my bases required to explain to you a reflected life. I have broken through the barriers of our current education infrastructures and come out on top. I have taken on society and won. Everything you have told me that I can not do I have done in a very short period of time. I have paved a way for a potential educational, sociological, theological, and philosophical revolution. The framework is now available to every human being on this planet to become more than they are if they so choose. All that is needed is for a few individuals to jump on board and our species is then headed for a new golden age. I have won because my work is done. With this consideration in mind, I no longer care about life. I have given you absolutely everything I have in me and you have taken the opportunity to bleed me dry. I fought against and defeated your ignorant understandings. I won by obtaining the self that you reject as impossible.

But I am a philosopher and am not without a plan. Even though I share the same fate as my predecessor, Saint Nietzsche, does not mean that I am out of cards. I have one card left up my sleeve. Maybe Nietzsche did as well but it was overlooked. Or maybe it was his destiny to prepare the path for me. Dearest Nietzsche, it was you who were the image of the divine. You never claimed yourself as a superman but instead created the foundations for us to understand what being a superman might entail. Despite all your physical and mental sickness, you were the most healthy of us all. You were always the first superman. I can only walk in your footsteps. And for this, I give you all of my honour for the last two courses. Your life offered more saintly fruits than any other declared saint that I have studied. I give you all my respect and gratitude my dear teacher. I see your halo that you present as horns.

The card up my sleeve is nothing more than simple addition. I have spent my life learning and therefore have accumulated such a vast understanding of things and the possibility for courses seem infinite. But you will get nothing more from me until you enable the necessary conditions in order to allow me to be who I am. I desire to help all of humanity to the best of my ability but you do not allow me to do this. This course on suicide is only an introduction to most of the topics that our human minds battle with. My course on life is only the manifold of some of the problems that we struggle with in this life. These topics journey much deeper and my own mind understands many of these perspectives well. I have countless courses travelling and building through my mind and the only question that remains is whether you want them or not. Even at this very moment I have the outlines of over ten courses prepared in my head ready for my pen to hit the paper. I have hundreds of courses only waiting for new material to make sense of their relations. Now let us do some basic mathematics considering the person that I am.

Let us say that I will only live thirty more years. Let us also assert that I only produce and release six educational courses a year to all of humanity via the Internet. This means that I would of produced over one hundred and eighty educational courses entirely free for everybody in the world to make use of. But you will not enable the conditions to allow me to carry out this noble pursuit. And my response is to do exactly what I am doing this very moment. Is adhering to your currency based systems really worth more than this?

So after countless attempts to rectify these issues, both you and your systems scream "no!" After many years of trying so hard to be the best that I could be for you people, your very spit reaches my face. I give absolutely everything that I have within myself to you and my only trophies to bring home are slimy and yellow. Seriously, why should I bother trying to make the world a better place? Your mucus tells a story. It is a representation of you.

In order to cope with your cruelty I will retreat into my own mind. I will be locked up in a room and refuse the application of speech, except for any black swans that I might discover. I will keep a notebook on my person and spend my time reflecting and studying. Notebook after notebook will be course after course ready for production. My life will be revolved around the desire to help our species, but only if it desires to help itself. These notebooks will pile up and be stored in a secure location. If I only complete one notebook per month, do your mathematics... And these notebooks will remain in vain if no one comes to claim them, that is me. The wasted potential as a result of our systems is exposed for exactly the same problems that I have been explaining to you throughout this course. I am holding myself as a hostage and the ransom is the only human necessity: love. When I obtain this, the courses will go into production and every human being will have the opportunity to benefit from what I have to offer. And all this is worth zero dollars and I am proud of that fact. To hand over the ability to find oneself is more precious than any of your coins. What is true value?

I could spend the rest of my life developing a sustainable model for the future of education. I know its follies from experience and I can fix them. I can implement donation optional based systems that encourage the best and most passionate teachers to invest their talents into the Internet. And you know what, even if I do not do it then eventually the poorly structured systems will do it but only corrupting the ideal: a cheap copy.

What is the value of this course to you? What about ten courses structured in a similar manner? What is the value of my own unique identity? How much is my life worth? Are you going to write this homeless warrior off as you do to all the others that you turn your head away from as you walk the streets? Is the opinion of one man just as valuable as another? Is the opinion of one man less valuable than the collective's? Is my own life really as worthless as you demonstrate to me?

Eleftheria i thanatos. Freedom or death.

ACT 19
DEAR SUICIDAL FRIEND
January 7, 2012

Dearest Fellow Sufferer,

In a world that seems to have forgotten the individual behind the skin, we become frightened of continued existence. The results of our past which has led us to our current undesired situations makes us feel bound to a particular mode of existence and we feel trapped within it. The ideal life that we desire seems impossible and it feels like you are the only one who cares. Abandoned by a world that has turned their backs, suicide becomes such a tempting escape. But in dealing with such matters, one should learn the specifics of this decision, as the permanent action is not one to be reversed. If we are to contemplate suicide, we should first learn what it is that we are speaking of.

This heartfelt letter to my fellow human companion has no other purpose than to assist your decision. It is in attempts to present these arguments in an objective fashion. For Do not live your life and it is not my place to judge your actions, for it is not your life that I live. As you were thrown into the world through no choice of your own, you were given one primary responsibility and that is yourself. It is you that is in control of your own vessel: if your suffering is so great that you must end your life, then I am not one to judge and neither is anyone else, even when they say they are. Suicide is a choice and it is not the intention of this letter to convince you of anything else. All that I ask is that you hear this letter out and grasp any wisdom that it might pass on to you. If you have or are contemplating suicide, then I encourage you to read and think about this letter. A decision as important as a life needs careful consideration and reflection before the act. You would not desire to realise any different after the damage has been inflicted. The slide to non-existence is frightening when one "wakes up" before death. I am writing from experience within this topic and I hope that you consider my words.

I would like you to know my credentials to speak of this subject. I have suffered from suicidal ideation for much of my life. My cries for help were constantly ignored and I had no idea where to turn. After much searching, I turned to philosophy. Philosophy is not a magical pill that can cure over night, however, philosophy can present many perspectives that can give us the tools to make ourselves, and dare I say our lives, into the ideal that we desire most in our hearts. And philosophy will help our hearts position their attachments to healthy and pure desires. I am not claiming that philosophy will rid you of your human condition, but what I am claiming is that it can help you bear it and investigate methods to overcome it. No, these methods will not be written in chronological order for you, for this medicine is one that is created by yourself. In actuality philosophy will make things worse before they get any better. But when one places suicide on the table, we are faced with the greatest of all philosophical questions, "to be or not to be". To transcend the problems that we have created in life we must first slay our dragons. To look our demons in the eyes in order to study them. And when we find the root of the problems we are then in the position to find ways to remove them from our lives.

At first we will cover the topic of the existential crisis. The feeling of hopelessness and alienation in an abysmal world. Our attempts to pull ourselves up from the precipice is a frightening task especially when there is no rope from the world to be found. Here is a rope.

Later, we will consider some of the reasons why one might consider suicide and analyse some of its philosophical implications. To consider the value of life in attempts to clean up the taboo minefield that society has crafted. We will attempt to explore the topic that you struggle with as well as diagnose whether or not your own struggles with life have a deeper seeded root. For when we place our life on the line, we all struggle with the same existential crisis. If you are suicidal, what harm can come from learning some of the details of our suffering? It is precisely a result of this suffering that we now stand on this bridge. I am not here to talk you down. Just to talk.

To end, we will discuss transcendence. This is our ability to overcome ourselves. This section will be the most important content of this letter to you, my dear suffering soul. We will explore what it means to go beyond the self, giving the control of life back to the subject, namely, You.

It is the strong who will survive, for it is not the purpose of this letter to present you with an easy way out. For living life is far from easy. However, it is the intention of this letter to lead you to a road that can be walked if you so choose. For in honest and open discussion about suicide, we need to remember the importance of the topic. Your own incline towards suicide is directed at a drastic action. And sometimes drastic actions are needed to re-orientate ourselves. This letter will not direct you back into the comforts of your old life, for it is obvious that life did not work for you. If this leap from your old life frightens you, I encourage you to at least finish reading this letter before you make any decisions. This is your life and you can live it (or take that life away) if you choose. But for now, sit back and attempt to detach from your life and yourself while I outline some important topics that I believe that you should consider.

Just one more thing before we begin my friend. By the very fact that you are contemplating this very question places you in the best and most receptive position possible to enable change. When one no longer desires to continue existence, they become more free than ever before. Right now my dear reader, you are in a much better spot than all the other sleep walkers in the world. For the one who contemplates suicide is waking up. You are given a glimpse into the importance of philosophy, for your existential question is all enclosed around it. This letter will attempt to serenade you out of your slumber. And once you have woken, you stand in a much better position to decide whether or not you should end your life. Please hold my hand and walk with me and I will introduce you to the wilderness of the human. Let's now clear up the fog of the taboo topic of suicide.

We are forcibly thrown into an existence that we never asked for. We are raised in a fashion that we have little say over. We are socially enframed by our caretakers primarily and the external world of cultural normalities secondarily. After birth we study the world in order to make sense of it all. Eventually we discover that feet go on the ground and hat goes on the head. We explore the confinements of gravity and how our bodies react being pulled to the core of the earth. We attempt to articulate that abstract feeling in our souls but find it difficult to communicate to the other occupants of the world and this makes us frustrated. Thus we immerse ourselves in the language of our culture in order to better communicate because we realise that our comforts increase the more we are able to utilise its practice. Even from this young age we demonstrate an amazing ability of dedication towards what is not. For it is always the grail that seems impossible that is most rewarding to accomplish in life. As Heidegger might say, we are always living ahead of ourselves.

As we get older we are passed on a set of guidelines to live by. We are told when to brush our teeth, when to go to school, and when to go to sleep. We acquire a class lifestyle that will likely be passed to future generations. The mundane of the world is placed on a pedestal, and we are required to endure or embrace the ways of our company. We are pushed upon others similar ages to us and are required to make friendships or retreat into solitude. And making friendships is no easy task especially when the thoughts of one person do not harmonise with the thought of the other. Meaningful thoughts are discouraged by adults finding them ridiculous. Slowly each child learns from their environment how to "correctly" comport themselves in the world and they then hit puberty.

Our developing bodies and minds cause us much frustration. We are overcome with urges to do things that would be considered inappropriate. Freud would attribute this to our suppressed child rearing especially in the matter of sexual expression. Our Darwinian nature shows itself fully for the first time as we develop into beings towards reproduction. Just as we once learned how to walk and speak, we now learn how to shave. But this time our emotions develop deeper. We learn the power of words and the emotional attachments that they hold. We abstractly learn our way around romantic love and may make and break hearts along the way, and others may make and break our own. We come to learn our bodies and vanity becomes our identification. The way we believe that we appear to others is who we believe we are, and this self-conception will determine how we are seen by others. It will result in our self-confidence and the way we hold ourselves. The difficulties within emotional life are introduced to us and we are required to find ways to cope with the roller coaster of life.

Once we are able to take control of our emotions we develop into young adults. We invest into a detail in life and attempt to make an occupation of it. We study what we are required to in order to obtain that employment that we so desire, or we may already be lost in the abyss of life and not yet know what to do. We are presented two roads in education: the long or the short. For many, the desire to take the quickest road possible seems very attractive, usually leaving its long term results repressed or unconsidered. Our hunger for freedom weighs heavy on our hearts and we believe that this freedom can be obtained by enslaving ourselves into employment as quickly as possible. For we have been at first ruled by our caretakers and now desire to break from that. We transition our enslavement from parental to employment and government. And according to our social normalities, this is when one "grows up".

Eventually we find solace in routine. We play the television repeats over and over again. We find resentment within employment and as Marx would likely say, we despise it because the fruits of our own labour is being exploited from us by another. Yet each day we muster up enough courage to wake ourselves up to bring our bodies to work. With little fulfilment being found in employment, we look around our lives to find something else to cling to, something else to fill the emptiness in our hearts. So we attempt to manifest this within family. We marry and have children, repeating this chicken and egg process. But this time we are on the other side of the coin.

We grow older while repeating the process of our caretakers. We love our children and desire the best for them, so we indoctrinate them with what we have found to be best. They grow older and we experience their lives with them. We see them grow and become very protective as we would anything that we deeply care for. The years go by and we learn from both our romantic relationships and our children. The mundane of employment becomes tolerable when the rest of our life seems to be fulfilling. The years race by and our children leave us. We might be proud of them but we invested so much of our lives into them that we are unsure how to let go. A new life presents itself to us and our direction is disorientated. To cope we may try new and different experiences, or we may retreat into the comforts and discomforts of loneliness. While our children are just beginning their journey, ours feels complete... or maybe incomplete.

We age and either become reflective in our years or immerse ourselves into hobbies. Our health deteriorates and our options reduce their scope. We slowly learn how to accept death and once we have been deemed too much of a hassle, we are administered into aged care homes. This is of course if we were lucky enough not to die by accident or of disease. Our children have children and we may be lucky enough to experience one or two future generations created from our own offspring. The process continues and we learn to rest in our coffin by seeing all the fruits of our lives. A life lived with the minimal purpose actualised: to endure through it to successfully reproduce the species.

Do you see anything wrong with this picture? For this is the circle of life. But how are we to find and create meaning in our own lives? For this picture of a human life is the one that most current cultures and societies have placed as purpose. In actual fact this is the purpose of the society that we are placed in and not our own. The deep seeded void that we feel is enslavement. Enslavement by society. For this picturesque life is handed down and not your own. Considering this, what purpose do you have? Have you yet found your own purpose or you still wallowing confined to the chains of the purpose of the state? If this question rings any bells for you, let me assure you that all hope is not lost no matter what your age. But my dear fellow human being, I am getting ahead of myself. Let us first discuss your predicament.

We begin our journey in the maze crying and wailing. Eventually we learn how to crawl around it exploring as one would explore the moon. When we learn to walk we take adventures to new dead ends. As we get older we realise this maze to be a method of travel and we remove ourselves from our situated place and begin to walk. We walk great distances time and time again only to find dead ends. We become frustrated in life, for it never seems to be how we desire it. And how do we desire it? For that remains an abstract that we have difficulties to articulate. The path chosen is simply due to experience. For we are in a struggle to actualise the life that we desire, and the life that we desire can only be found through the experience and directions that we set ourselves on. As Hume might say, we must have experience before we are able to include that experience in our understandings. The life that we desire remains an unknown until that life is actualised. Therefore, life is but a game and it is us that must make our move, and after doing so stand back to watch the results of that move. The present is but a means to the future, and the past is our history book to learn from.

We therefore stand on the precipice of the mountain staring into the abyss of what could be. The feeling is daunting and our natural instinct is to step away from the edge. For when one looks down, they are not looking into the world but themselves. The possibilities within the self seems infinite but at the same time futile. When one no longer values their own life within their particular environment and community, that edge is such a beautiful spot to sit. For the abyss is so attractive to the suffering soul. For one not only has the ability to throw themselves off but also can choose where to throw themselves off. My fellow sufferer, it is not the intention of this letter to ask you to step away from the edge, actually quite the opposite. But it is instead the intention of this letter to equip you with the understanding to wisely make the choice as to where you could throw yourself into that said abyss.

Even though the precipice gives us comforts in our darkest hours, it also causes us pain. What could be taunts us and we can only seem to visualise it from afar. The magnificent mountain decreases its beauty the closer we get to it. The agitation of living in the present and striving towards the future wears away our endurance. We feel alone and alienated in a world that shows little or no concern for the particular individual but instead places its eggs in the basket of the collective. Unhealthy relationships are looked over and we feel trapped within them. We come to understand true loneliness independent of whether people are around or not. For you are not the same breed as those sleep walkers my friend. There is something in you that embraces purpose and meaning, otherwise I would not be speaking to you while you stand on that cliff. This despair that we feel is what Kierkegaard calls anxiety. And it is within this anxiety that we are most perceptive to see the chains on our wrists. Look at your chains my friend. For it is these chains that have led you to the edge of the cliff.

Who are you? Is your body you? Your thoughts or actions? Locke suggests that there is no thing in itself but only properties of those things. For example, try and describe a tree without its properties. The tree is a tree because it possesses the "treeness" of a tree. Without these properties there is no tree. This is similar to Buddha's onion, for we are but layers enclosed in nothing. And it is that nothing that truly is. In addition, one can never truly see a tree but only a certain perspective of the tree. Our human make-up does not allow us to truly perceive the tree in its entirety, but only gives us a snapshot from a certain perspective: we assume the rest.

Sartre expounds on this nothingness by relation to a coffee shop. You arrange to meet your friend there and you look around and see nothing, for the one you are looking for is nowhere to be seen. You sit down and wait for them, all the while filtering out what is, in search for what is not, namely, your friend. Thus this time, and maybe time and time again before you have given up on finding your true desires because your search for what is not has failed again and again.

Again I am not telling you to step away from the edge fellow suffering comrade. But please hear my words before you make that leap of faith. But let me assure you that there is hope. My proposition is by far not an easy road to travel, but nothing great happened over night. The path will give you appreciation for the life that you wish to make for yourself. Through the journey you will find and create meaning, forever forming your own destiny. For the more that you experience and learn, the more that your ideal life will change. You will become master of your own destiny and shape this world to suit yourself, instead of allowing the world to shape you. Human purpose is to surpass the limits of itself. Let us start with your chains...

How would you do it? What method would you utilise to end your life? Would you cut yourself and bleed out, jump from a precipice, throw yourself in front of a moving vehicle, poison or overdose yourself, hold yourself under water, stick a gun to the side of your head, or starve or dehydrate yourself? How much violence and suffering are you willing to withstand to carry out the deed? When one decides to fade from this world this becomes and important question. And most importantly, could your act stand as a universal allowance given to all mankind? If a loved one was to perform the act that you are thinking of, would it be okay? What moral responsibility do you have regarding your own life? Kant suggests that we must first consider our actions in relationship to the universal in order to carry out a just act. For example, lying would be immoral because we ourselves do not wish for others to lie to us. Thus lying is an immoral action because it cannot be made universal. If you are to perform the act, you should first consider as many perspectives as you can. Remember the permanence of this action. There is no undo button and if we are in error, we should identify it before we make decisions without an undo button.

Let us picture a world inhabited by unthinking automatons. Where each is stuck in their own programming, carrying out actions that they have conditioned their conscious to perform. This world is semi-functional as a collective, but when the individual is questioned as to why they do the things they do they are unable to answer sufficiently. If a question out of the "ordinary" is presented to one of these automatons, they become uneasy, for their way of life has just been questioned. The reasons for their actions is not consciously known and they become defensive to protect their way of life which the spotlight has just shined. The easiest solution is to remove the one "disrupting the peace" and that is exactly what happened. The one posing the questions was Socrates. The one now posing the questions is U.

For the one who no longer clings to life is not in as bad as position as they think. For suicidal ideation is but the birthing pains of a truly magnificent soul that is waking from their slumber. That soul is you and I hope that you continue to read and absorb my words. For they are written for you and come from the bottom of my heart. Let my song encourage you to open your eyes after a lifetime of sleep. It is you that I want by my side and not those who are addicted to their sleeping pills. It is time to rise my friend. Let me help you to your feet. When you rise let us dance together, but remember that it takes two to tango. It is not the intention of this letter to bring you back to the point where you can once again cling to life, for this is one of the follies of mankind, for clinging itself causes us suffering. It is your suicidal state that gives you power, for your life is no longer of concern. By this seeded desire for death has already brought you outside the box of the collective. Now I urge you to follow my words so that you can now learn to transcend your current suffering. Mankind is something to surpass. Are you up for the task? What do you have to loose? You are already contemplating ending it all. And that is why anything is possible with you my friend.

In order to repair a car one must first identify the root cause for the malfunction. Similarly, to fix your computer one must first find out what is causing your computer to act up. Humans are not so different in so far as we have underlying issues for the problems that we experience. This is why Western medicine can be extremely dangerous because so often it is only the symptoms that are being treated. If you fix your car with some tape or fix your computer by going around the problem leaves your equipment vulnerable to not only not taking care of the problem, but also will most likely make it worse or even cause new problems. The person that you have made yourself into to date can be explained not only from your past and your hereditary genes, but also in the history of the world that you were brought in to. To track back these causes both helps you to understand yourself and gives you direction as to where you might go in order to rectify these issues.

Thus, if you choose not to end your life then direction is given. To attempt to articulate the abstract of your own consciousness becomes your task. For this is no easy mission and failure after failure will result. But in each failure we reach success. In these pursuits we place ourselves on a staircase and if we make it happen we can travel up more often then down. Each failure as a step, because in each failure you get closer to the ideal that you search for. There exist very few situations in which we are able to leap over many stairs. One cannot leap over their own shadow. Make friends with your shadow, for it will remind you of what you once thought to be the "real world". Isn't it about time you wake up? You my friend are not your shadow.

If it is oneself that is not liked then one needs to find and work on the underlying reasons behind that. If it is the environment that is found problematic, one needs to take steps to change that. And if it is social relationships that cause suffering, repair or recreation is what is needed. One is never stuck in a situation. There is always ways out. To turn your back and walk away from it all is always an option. You are always where you place yourself to be. If all else fails, use your feet and walk away. For this solution can save a precious life. To repair and recreate, one needs a healthy atmosphere. It is you that are required to make that atmosphere. To turn around and start walking is sometimes the best solution. Your people are out there. You just have to find them. And I assure you that what you will be leaving is only a conglomerate of sleeping souls. For now I suggest that you stand up, stretch your arms, yawn, and prepare yourself for the road ahead.

"Why me?" you might ask. And I will tell you my friend. You are but a subject of evolution. Imagine a species of black butterflies that have brought into the world a minority of mutated offspring, this offspring being white. The atmospheric conditions are not appropriate for these butterflies as they are easily spotted by birds who would love to eat them. As a response, the strongest must fight for their survival. One of these white butterflies embarks on a journey for survival and travels up a mountain. This mountain is covered with snow and it is now the black butterflies that become the main course on the birds menu. Thus the white butterfly transcends its dietary problem. This mutated trait now becomes an advantage and is now envied by its fellow species. It is now this characteristic that other butterflies desire and the population is only to thrive if the mutation is passed on to offspring. Darwin might say that it is suffering that can inspire an entity to change its situation. But this butterfly was something special as it pushed on in its suffering to change its existence. You can be this butterfly. But with that being said, our comforts make us lazy. It was only this one butterfly that was able to act on the world instead of having the world act on it. The rest of the butterflies were merely sleeping. This, my friend, is your wake up call.

Thus our project in life becomes focused on the conditions that we suffer from so that we may no longer suffer. According to Nietzsche, the human is something to surpass. He presented to us an ideal of human that is worthy and meaningful to strive for. A human that creates their lives in the way that they understand best. Not a being that falls on dogmatics but instead one who creates their own morality as well as their own life. Nietzsche's project was that of the over-man to overcome mankind. And it is the demons in your own life that must be overcome. Just as in repairing a car, we need to identify and learn these demons before we have any chance to go beyond them. For when your demons become known, they fade away into the background, no longer important. To know ourselves is to understand what we can from ourselves and the world.

Do we have to suffer? Tolle suggests that we do not, for the only reason for our suffering is rooted in our thoughts that we should not have to suffer. While one suffers, they suffer because they believe that they should not suffer. For when one sheds this erroneous assumption and embraces or accepts suffering, the term "suffering" becomes incomprehensible. Suffering makes no sense without its bearer desiring to not suffer. The idea of suffering collapses when one accepts all that is and becomes without resentment. Thus, suffering is but an attitude created by our desire to not suffer. One might have to walk through overgrown prickly bushes before arriving at their destination. We must first walk through the valley of the shadow of death before we are to find green pastures. And as I said before, sometimes one must go down before going up.

What is this path that I present to you? It is the path directed towards health. It is the road to meaning and greater understanding. It is the drastic wake up call to your own life and your purpose within such a massive world. It is the road of the philosopher. For it is in our search to find ourselves that we are able to find the life that is best suited to us. To choose any different is to accept the unacceptable. And I know you do not accept this because you are ready to end your life. Instead, why not search for the divinity found within yourself so that you may share your best possible self with those around you. For if you give your all to make yourself into the best person that you can be, you no longer have regrets to worry about. And if you put your all into this task, you are in turn becoming the best that is possible: a perfect you. And it is through your divine self that you will attract your people.

So now I come to an end of this letter of love and care. You are now presented with choices which you may have not previously realised. Because you have read this you are now in a different position than you were. And this is the same with all philosophy, for when greater understanding is achieved, our possibilities increase and we are better prepared to make difficult decisions. I appreciate your time and persistence and you are now set free back into the world of your own reality with things to think about and plans to make. If you do decide to end your life, I hope it goes how you desire it. If you decide to run back to the comforts of your own miserable existence, then I also hope you fair well with that, however, I believe the results to be similar to suicide. For when greater understanding is achieved, it becomes part of you and you are then given a responsibility. You will not lose this letter because it has now become a part of you. And it is precisely this that makes the human so wonderful. You will always be more than you are, for we are beings of constant development. This is why each conscious second is so important. They are seconds that we are able to fine tune and develop in the most efficient way possible. Each second passes us and we are asked, "What of it?" And we have the option to reply, "To become more then I am." Have you gotten out of bed yet?

With Love (Blood),

Wendell Charles NeSmith

P.S. What next? From here I will direct you to the book, "Sophie's World" by Jostein Gaarder. Welcome to philosophy my friend. Let us both create a meaningful life.

[See, I have always been after your daughter's Heart.]

ACT 20
BEYOND SICKNESS
September, 2011

What does it mean to be "sick"? Am I sick? Mental Health Australia answers yes to that question. If I am sick, then what is everybody else? Healthy?

How we to make our way in the world in a healthy manner? What can we do about our own sickness? How are we to overcome the darkness of our own minds? How can we repaint the blemishes on the artwork called life?

Our human condition. It is our cross which every man must carry if they are to stay true to themselves. It stands as our weakness which debilitates our content attitude within the world. It stands as a roadblock to where we wish to be. It is the box which we are trapped within. How is one to overcome the impossible? It is our life project which most ignore or fail. How is one to paint their own life to represent their own found beliefs and understandings? To mould the clay in the way that we desire it. We are given a vessel, and through that vessel we must first gain control of it in order to get where we want to be.

A mountain climber in the world. Questioning everything that seems strange and unusual. Learning from all that is given and making something new from it. To climb a mountain one must sometimes go down in order to get further up. To realise our follies and learn to transcend them. To accurately make judgements about the world so that we can overcome the problems within the world.

Existing amongst the deaf. How are we to communicate? Are the current desires within our heart possible? If not, how can we transcend them? Are we on the right path? If not, what can reorientate us? A preacher without an audience is ineffective. But what must be overcome is precisely the present - the current struggles. If one desires to move a ball with only their mind, no amount of time may accomplish this. Our priorities must be rearranged and our methods adapted, possibly time and time again. As climbing an unknown mountain, we remain unsure of what we might face. It would be ludicrous to stagnate at a particular stage of the journey - to give up the journey which has so far been travelled. Our aim remains to overcome the road blocks so that we may finish our journey.

To push our boulder up our mountain. It is easier said than done. One has two choices in life. To find a set of beliefs and understandings and follow them, or for one to make their own path. To exist as a member of the herd or to wander away from the herd and act instead of watch. If one chooses the latter, they take the weight of the world on their shoulders by themselves. They become like Atlas, carrying their boulder through the thick and thin of life. Tall overgrowth stands in our way. One has to not only clear it but also bring their enormous cross with them. Their luggage is enough to drive one mad, and if they become mad, their boulder remains. To travel the created road of life existing as a madman carrying a boulder becomes the stray's responsibility.

And what of the madman's loneliness? To choose the otherwise of society's given options leads away from people. To wander off from the herd is to leave the group behind. To make a new path is to travel a lonely road, one where others have not been and will probably not follow. To break free of one's chains ironically chains social relationships. To exist as the philosopher who steps outside of the box is to exist outside of what is comfortable. The weight of the boulder becomes heavier and results as alienation by chasing one's peripheral vision. Relationships will fall and so will its bearer. To take on the road to healing our sickness will result in more closely understanding and experiencing our sickness. To follow the heart to Africa to help the unfortunate will result in experiencing and observing those unfortunate. To find a cure we will first find many failures. For support will be difficult if not impossible to obtain. Is the philosopher not in a Catch-22. For they are damned if they do and they are damned if they do not. For few souls wish to be alone. As Aristotle said, "For without friends, no one would choose to live, though he had all other goods". But for one to carry their cross requires for them to put their highest good before their comforts. To live a life that perfectly paints your journey is to live through that journey.

To be human is to be unhuman. We all exist as subjective beings who perceive the world in slightly different ways. We see things that others cannot, choose not, or have not seen. We are given a conscious awareness and asked what we are to do with it. For most ignore it. Others attempt to study it from an objective point of view, dissociating from it. And the few, speaking of Nietzsche's few, see something that seems out of place that deserves their full attention. As a child might ask, "What is life?", and the adult laughs at them and diverts their question. It is the philosopher that holds on to these questions and refuses to let them drift into the background. To question the human condition is to stand apart from the human. To focus on what makes us human, and what our "condition" is, ironically makes us unhuman. For the human is not to question these things but accept them. Mob mentality becomes the more accurate description of the human, and one is either with them or against them. Those who have strayed from the herd to search for their medicine to combat their condition are seen as the enemy, and thus treated as such.

To mould one's life into who they are is the task of the philosopher. To transcend their own conditions becomes their life goal. To carry their boulder to the top of the mountain is their objective. As Socrates struggled with the concept of knowledge, he articulated his life to question what we really know. As Kierkegaard struggled with anxiety, he poetically drew us a picture systematically analysing its manifestation. As Nietzsche was physically and mentally weak, he composed a symphony of power. We all have reasons why we do the things that we do, but it is the few who dedicate their all to overcome what seems impossible. And ironically, it is from these "nonhumans" that we can truly learn what it means to be a human.

Be yourself. It has been said that someone can be anything that they want to be. That is entirely untrue. We live in a caste system and our choices are limited. Not only that, one who is frightened of blood cannot be a doctor. Nor would one who has a phobia of the telephone work in a call centre. In retrospect, one can only ever be what they are. What we can choose, however, is to what extent we going to explore ourselves. Are we going to ignore the monster in the corner of our eye or investigate it? It is this monster that the philosopher has stared in their own eyes, learning how to defeat. To be astute in life is their objective - to figure out ways to break through the wall in front of them. One will always be who they are (or shall I say become who they are) - the only question that remains is to what degree are you going to be yourself?

The plank in your eye. My question to you my dear reader, what plank is in your eye? I implore you to investigate what it is that you truly see in front of you, as I assure you things are not as you are told they are. Look for the monster in your own life and keep turning your head until you are able to stare it in its eyes. Learn this monster in and out, because it is this monster who is your opponent in life; your life project. Your life mission is to paint your existence the way that you see it, the way that you are and the way that you desire to be - your theme. Anything short of this is a contradiction of the self. To sacrifice the self on account of the world. As Hannah Arendt stated, "Better to be at odds with the whole world than to be at odds with the only one you are forced to live together with when you have left company behind." If you walk away from your destiny, you will be sleeping in the bed you made. As Jesus says in Luke 9:25 (NRSV), "What does it profit them if they gain the whole world, but lose or forfeit themselves?" I will incur and endure my alienation and rejection for the sake of my soul. Will you?

ACT 21
LOVE BASED LEARNING

To: jeremy.shearmur@anu.edu.au
Date: November 20, 2012, 2:48 PM

Dear Jeremy,

My name is Wendell Charles NeSmith and I am interested in transferring from Murdoch to ANU to complete my BA in Philosophy in aims to one day receive support for my thesis on love based learning. My entire life has been invested into this project. My entire life has been invested into philosophy and before you try and debunk this fact, let me explain to you the background conditions of me.

I suffer from Delayed Sleep Phase Disorder. I rarely sleep. Even as a child I was a philosopher because I would spend all of my time contemplating the most difficult subjects of all human existence. Each second presented me with an ethical dilemma: what should I do? The one streamed sleepless life became one in books. The clock never resets for me. So I dominate it by investing all of it into meaningful pursuits.

To begin with, from the very beginning this type of life alienated me from everyone else. So I spent my life searching for people who would love someone like me, which are few and far between. But this made me learn what love is or could be. Love is my focus in life and and always has been. How to integrate wisdom into society is what I was called to do, whether or not I end up benefiting from it. There are countless works backing up the words that I speak and I do hope you click some buttons to see who has just emailed you.

I am an online philosophy teacher attempting to revolutionise education by creating a loving learning environment on the Internet that will one day replace our current education systems. My father is a professor in education and I learned very well the errors of his ways through the practical failures that I observed within his own understandings.

I also attempt to revolutionise our mass media by presenting philosophy in an entertaining way. I have just finished a mythology movie about Pygmalion, aka, me. This will be released later this year and is my best and most controversial work. If I calculated correctly, this film will cause a chain reaction for our education and entertainment industries. And I have spent the last six or so years calculating this, for I am working around the Mayan calendar and this first movie will be released the day after the world ends. The movie attempts to romance a young girl into philosophy. You would not believe the miracles that I caught on camera. It is about to change a lot of hearts and the way people feel about philosophy. And I hope it to encourage young people to take philosophy more seriously.

I am an eccentric guy. I have spent the last two years travelling around Australia homeless, living in the wilderness. The last seven months has been living around the mountains of Canberra with my beautiful animal friends. I am poor and everything that I do, I do for free for the future evolution of our human society.

I am obsessed with the ideal of a utopian society. I have studied its theory for my entire life and I have everything that it takes to start a chain reaction that will one day obtain us one. And my works speak for themselves. I am famous for them. But because I deviated from a typical "university" education and instead focused everything on self-development, not for a degree, but for the result of the human that I become, "academics" will not even look at my work. But my work is based upon solid foundations and I am ready for them to argue about any of the subjects that I have released to the public... Public use of reason, go Kant! I am fulfilling your prophesy. You just did not have the Internet to make it happen. I will bring you enlightenment.

I want to transfer from Murdoch to ANU. I have almost completed the degree there but I would prefer to move into ANU for everything. I was not happy with Murdoch and that is why I am in Canberra. My life directed me to the ANU philosophy department for a reason and I am doing my best to jump through all of the loops to help me get my thesis right, for it will be my baby.

I want to be an ANU student and I would like to be directed to the quickest path for me to get help with a thesis on love based learning. I have studied all of my life but will do whatever units that you want me to so that I can be a part of ANU. Ultimately, one day, I would love to be employed by you guys. You can not get more of a philosophy nut than me and having the world's most passionate philosopher on your team who is already famous for his work would be beneficial for both of us.

I want to apply but there is a fee that I am unable to afford. I could afford it on a payment plan or I could just save up and apply for it late and pay the late fee. I am homeless so money like this is money that is taken away from my stomach. But I need to be here. The problem that I see with all of this is I am afraid to fork out the money and then be rejected by you. Philosophy is my life. Please help me make it my life within the ANU structures.

I have spent my lonely life travelling around the world and I came to Australia's heart for ANU. At first I wanted friends but I quickly realised that these departments tend to not possess nor care about love with their employment. But after much consideration I have realised that I should be in this school and I could really use the help to create a solid thesis that will be highly respected by all academic fields. And the thing is, is this thesis has already been completed through many different formats publicly available. But my next step needs to be to create an academic researched based format of this thesis. I am ready to start right now, I want to start right now, but I will jump through all of your hoops to become "the person" that you guys want me to be in order to receive your help for this altruistic life investment.

Please do get back to me as soon as possible. I would love to meet with you and discuss potential future plans. I am really looking for an "in". I love ANU and want it to be my home. Please help me make it my home by helping me open the doors required to do the philosophy that I was built for. I am ready to become ANU's most dedicated philosopher and I have a sleepless life full of conscious seconds to give it all to. And I always shine brightly as the star that I am for all of the world to recognise my origin, which could one day be you. Please help this flower to bloom so that you can display it proudly to the world.

With Heart,

Wendell Charles NeSmith
nesmith.net

From: Jeremy Shearmur
Jeremy.Shearmur@anu.edu.au

To: Wendell Charles NeSmith
Cc: Kate Achilles
daniel.nolan@anu.edu.au
Date: November 20, 2012, 4:09 PM

Dear Wendell,

Thanks for your e-mail and all the information about yourself.

At the ANU, issues about admission and transfer are handled externally, and then by our College administrators, rather than by academic staff, so I can't assist you directly. In addition, at ANU there is no BA in Philosophy - the best that one can do is to pursue philosophy within the B.A. degree (or within one or other of our combined degrees).

To submit an undergraduate application to ANU you'd need to apply through the University Admissions Centre: http://www.uac.edu.au/

For information about applying for the Bachelor of Arts, and

undertake a major in Philosophy, see:
http://studyat.anu.edu.au/programs/3111XBARTS;overview.html

I'm sending a copy of my note to you to one of our administrators, and also to the Deputy Head of our program, who looks after undergraduate issues for us, in case you need to be in touch with either of them.

All good wishes

Jeremy

To: Jeremy Shearmur
Date: November 20, 2012, 8:16 PM

Thanks for your reply Jeremy. I am only interested in a BA in philosophy. So I have enrolled back in Murdoch to finish my degree via correspondence.

When I finish then could a door open for me as a PhD student at ANU? Do I need to finish with an honours?

I am not going to lie. I hate our current university structures. It is all about who you know, how well you follow instructions, and how well you fit in with the herd. I care about virtue. I care about the good life and how to live it. I don't waste my time breaking apart theories without any practical application. I so want to one day be a PhD student at ANU, but I know that I will not fit in with that crowd. And I think that this combined with my rebellion against our current employment of education (without love) would hurt my chances. But I would be happy to be the recluse of the group. I wouldn't bother anyone. I would just do my work and stay to myself.

All of my work is very controversial. This will not change, for my methods are from the god responsible for the death of Pentheus, for this goat drives my spirit. Would the ANU PhD program even consider someone like me? My entire life is the love of wisdom, and this became my primary obsession in life even as far back into childhood as I can remember. And all of it I have been trying to fit myself in to society. Please say that a career for someone like me is possible at ANU. I am who I am. And I have so much to give to society if your doors would open up to me.

I am always personal because I can only live one life. I am unable to act how schools want me to act because my life is all entangled in these subjects. And I am very emotional and this also does not help me in your university's systems. But I am who I am and if systems like yours refuse me then they are the ones responsible for my homelessness. Because philosophy is not my occupation but my life. And if an eccentric genius is excluded for these reasons, then I question the ethics behind the systems. I am not going anywhere and exclusion from my entire life's investments just because I am weird could prove Darwin wrong (or maybe right).

My main fields of expertise are love, education, virtue ethics, mythology, sociology, and collective psychology - just in case this makes a difference. And my whole life is dedicated to these topics.

To: Wendell Charles NeSmith
Date: November 22, 2012, 7:28 AM

Dear Wendell,

Thanks for your note; I hope that your BA goes well.

As for the ANU, you need to bear in mind the *kind* of philosophy that it done here. It - and our graduate students - are typically doing high-powered rather narrowly analytical work, and there is now normally a requirement that people are doing that, if they are to be admitted.

Jeremy

To: Jeremy Shearmur
Date: November 25, 2012, 6:49 PM

Dear Jeremy,

I found a part in society that my soul cares so deeply for that I have given my life to protect and nourish it. I think that teaching is much more receptive when it is administered with love, care, and particularity. I am convinced that actually caring about those you teach can provide the best level of education to our future society.

I want to spend the rest of my life demonstrating how all of these structures could be developed to improve global consciousness about important topics.

My question to ANU is whether they would think about supporting and helping me research and write a really good thesis about making open source education a sustainable model of education with basic level options free to the entire world to obtain a university grade and better education system.

I am demonstrating how it could all work in Divine Tragedy's first film Ivory Heart that will be released at the end of the year. nesmith.net, targeted at children and teens.

This is my life project and I would really appreciate guidance as to how I could obtain educational achievement success throughout my life travels that take me through amazing philosophical journey's.

Wendell

To: Wendell Charles NeSmith
Date: November 25, 2012, 7:43 PM

Dear Wendell,

There are different styles in which philosophy is done, and I'd strongly suggest that you check out the *kind* of work that is currently done by people at the ANU - which I'd describe as for the most part, rather narrowly analytical and technical.

Given the *kind* of thing on which you wish to work, I can't see that applying to the ANU would be likely to be a very fruitful thing to do. As I explained, what is required of our incoming students, is that they undertake work in analytical philosophy; and while if people's interests lie in that area, it is a great setting within which to work, if they don't, then there is very little on offer.

All good wishes

Jeremy

To: Jeremy.Shearmur@anu.edu.au
Date: November 26, 2012, 3:10 AM

I have read the thesis of multiple PhD graduates of yours.

My problem still, is that I wish to do careful analytical research on why this type of learning is much more effective than our traditional learning atmosphere. I plan on learning from many different types of people in test situations that would give us sociological insight.

The "type" of philosophy that I do is the type originally meant for academic learning. I was not asking ANU for assistance with the entire range, but part of, which is assistance to obtain empirical researched based evidence to support or reject my premises.

If ANU would not be a good candidate furthering my future education, then who would after my BA? I am very serious about these topics and will be spending my life on them. And I am in the education system whether or not my methods are traditional.

The next few years of my life is being planned out to make mythological documentary films around the beautiful ACT. People will know if educational institutions reject me and that would reflect the "kind" of philosophy that they do.

Wendell

To: Wendell Charles NeSmith
Date: November 26, 2012, 8:30 AM

Dear Wendell,

The situation at ANU has changed: the old department in the Faculty of Arts has merged with the RSSS department, and the new graduate students working here fit the interests and concerns of the people in the old Research School (as well as a few people working on contemporary French 'continental' philosophy). They are simply not doing the kind of thing that you are wishing to do.

Jeremy

WORDS OF WISDOM
December 31, 2013 - January 1, 2014

Love is the only answer to our human problems. Throughout my adventures, I have discouraged many who dreamed of a day where they could make "a lot of money" so they could "help a lot of people" with it. I have spent my life meeting people. I know people very well and this approach does not work. It dooms its pursuer to living an unsuccessful life of Satan worshipping. Money belongs to those who create it, and when those who do force me to use it, then we have a problem.

You have been raised in a sinful world. Below its mask you will come to realise that our species can be in no worse state. Meaningless conscious activity wasted away in order to cope with its external pressures. Truly never being able to fit in because in order to do that, one must devote themselves to its congregation and their alignments. The only survivors being those who ignore their game and make up their own. This in turn being very risky with a high chance of failure. The odds of our motivations to try and live upright are stifled by the taunts of their audience.

But we are destined for greatness because a new species will soon be born. The betwixed and between will soon rule as the fairy dust is distributed as pages administered into the mind's eye. Half human and half angel, the divine blood will command rule. And when the results of compassionate life toils unfold, our society will be required to respond. And from their failures to adequately answer, the species will be cut in two. Those who act will become kings by right: what they naturally do. The world is about to become a stage for the bravest of warriors. We will both laugh and cry with the information we will uncover over the next ten years. Because our new leaders are individuals who God has selected to administer Its Will upon the population. Those who are this will be this. If one is called to devote their entire life into a field of philanthropy, that is what they are going to do whether you like it or not. To kill the genetic mutation is the only way to prevent it from being what it is. And when you do that, you merely light trails of fire that will release wrath upon your own kind.

Love based learning is the only way to truly teach an Other. All of the systems we have now follow rules and regulations that make it impossible for any teacher to do that. Thus the students end up not enjoying their studies. As a result, only their youth is spent learning. An occupation acquired, the memory enables us to learn its day to day expectations. We then turn our senses off and eventually become dull in our trinity of perception. The end of the journey starts when you "grow up" so I hope you are ready to waste your life like everybody else. Or you could do something different. If you are unable to find your ideal teacher, become it.

What is a musician? One who analyses its waves is its technician. One who slices them into pieces to rearrange them, its doctors. But those who do both sing its hymns. For music can be understood and interpreted within all aspects of life. And its beauty: decay. The note struck always being its intended target, whether or not the audience warmly receives it. But either way, Its tones are very vibrant within me and all that I interact with. I see music playing out in life so I sing those hidden stories through many formats, and soon to be music. But from the start of the race, I was always a musician. Whether I make a course, film, tv show, book, or record; the truth is that the events that produced its output are musical in nature and that can be clearly examined from its beginnings. Poetry of the heart will both sevr and unite our species. The bard is now back and this time, for good. Your attempts to remove my kind from your gene pool was not accepted lightly by the gods. They are coming back to punish the sinful and bless their disciples. They blessed us with Pandora to deliver us a message. Now we are at the end of her jar.

If you are going to dedicate your time to study under another, then that other must have your convicted respect. If their own lives do not clearly demonstrate that they are very wise in the fields of life that you desire to learn about, then why are you bothering with them? Just because your parents stick you in front of them means nothing. You have two feet. Do not learn from another who does not love within their teachings. I can assure you that they will only teach you what you need to know how to avoid. And mistakes in foundations takes great toils later to beautify.

The schooling systems that your parents force you within is evil. Teachers who have a good heart will eventually be corrupted. The amount of students they are required to babysit ensures the destruction of any ideals of change. It generates robots to generate robots.

What each and every one of you need is to live in a self sustaining community on a very large property. Your teachers are your tutors and they spend their lives walking around the community, teaching all who are interested in learning. From the unique abilities that you were blessed with, you will be led to trails that can teach not only those subjects to you, but also every other one. Every single is the same. And when we learn one obtaining its conceptual understanding, we will then be able to apply similar principles to all singles.

What you need for your new utopian society is me. Or at least someone like me. How backwards is our society to provide a world of opportunities for those who study a single field but reject those who study all of them, despite their significant contributions to each one of them. To discourage a polymath is stupid and will always backfire. Whether or not their methods are conventional, exclusion from its practice will not be tolerated. Because you all need me. You need me to show you how to show others. You need a spiritual leader who also reigns over their mental and physical. Your job is to appoint the best person for the job who can tutor your entire community into eudaimonia. It takes a special sort of person to lead us all to victory. To assume responsibility individually. Place the world on the shoulder's of those worthy. Let that worthy individual be U. Become Its sacrifice.

If you are to learn, learn Love, for it teaches all things. And if its messenger has no heart, then find one that does. Then Become It.

www.ingramcontent.com/pod-product-compliance
Lightning Source LLC
Chambersburg PA
CBHW070426290526
45791CB00005B/1851